THE JUNGLE SURVIVAL

POCKET MANUAL 1939–1945

Edited by Alan Jeffreys

CASEMATE

Philadelphia & Oxford

Published in Great Britain and
the United States of America in 2017 by
CASEMATE PUBLISHERS
The Old Music Hall, 106–108 Cowley Road, Oxford OX4 1JE, UK
1950 Lawrence Road, Havertown, PA 19083, USA

Introduction and chapter introductory texts by Alan Jeffreys
© Casemate Publishers 2017

Hardback Edition: ISBN 978-1-91086-021-2
Paperback Edition: ISBN 978-1-61200-436-5
Digital Edition: ISBN 978-1-61200-437-2

A CIP record for this book is available from the British Library

Printed in the Czech Republic by FINIDR, s.r.o.

The information and advice contained in the documents in this book is solely for
historical interest and does not constitute advice. The publisher accepts no liability for the
consequences of following any of the advice in this book.

For a complete list of Casemate titles, please contact:

CASEMATE PUBLISHERS (UK)
Telephone (01865) 241249
Fax (01865) 794449
Email: casemate-uk@casematepublishers.co.uk
www.casematepublishers.co.uk

CASEMATE PUBLISHERS (US)
Telephone (610) 853-9131
Fax (610) 853-9146
Email: casemate@casematepublishers.com
www.casematepublishers.com

Cover design by Katie Gabriel Allen

CONTENTS

'What a jungle trail at the front looks like'
Howard Brodie, 1942/3. *(Library of Congress)*

INTRODUCTION

The word 'jungle' is Indian in origin meaning 'wasteland' but it has been used to describe anything from sparsely covered wood areas to tropical forest. Until the Second World War, the jungle was usually described as bush or forest in military circles. Generally there are two types of jungle. Primary jungle defined as natural jungle growth with poor visibility and little undergrowth. Secondary jungle was cleared primary jungle that had re-grown and usually comprised dense undergrowth that severely limited movement.

The jungle was a terrifying alien environment for nearly all British, American, Australian, African and Indian troops during the Second World War as Lieutenant General (later Field Marshal) W. J. 'Bill' Slim, Fourteenth Army Commander, stated in a note on jungle fighting: 'it bewilders, depresses and even frightens us'. The jungle was beset with the problems of difficult climate, terrain, vegetation, wildlife and tropical disease such as malaria, typhus and cholera. Added to these were the tactical limitations imposed by the jungle: limited observation and fields of fire, communication problems, lack of mobility and long supply lines. As Slim wrote:

> The strangeness, the silence broken by a sudden unexplained noise, the limited visibility, the appalling laboriousness of movement, the knowledge that there is no 'front' and above all the isolation that you feel only a few yards from your comrades, will all affect you in the jungle at first. ('A note on Jungle Fighting in Burma', *Notes from Theatres of War* 19)

Thus troops fighting in South East Asia and the South West Pacific Area (SWPA) had to overcome terrain, the climate and the disease before they even considered the enemy.

The Japanese too were apprehensive of the jungle, as shown by this pamphlet issued to troops going overseas:

A dense forest, where wood, weeds and brambles intertwine ten and twenty fold is called a jungle. It is a haunt of savage beasts, poisonous snakes and noxious insects. The passage of the army is extremely difficult, and it is necessary to form a special operation party when passing through the jungle. However, such a natural feature is unsuitable for infirm Europeans, and in order to out-manoeuvre them it is very often necessary to break through the jungles. (*National Archives WO 208/1426*)

This book explores the experience of Western armies learning to operate and fight in the jungles of Asia in the Second World War through the training material produced for jungle warfare, in particular the experience of the British and Indian Armies in Burma. They suffered the most humiliating series of defeats in British and Imperial history as Hong Kong, Malaya (modern-day Malaysia), Borneo, Singapore and Burma (modern-day Myanmar) fell in rapid succession to the Imperial Japanese Army (IJA) in 1941 and 1942. Three years later the IJA suffered its worst defeat to date at the hands of the Fourteenth Army in Burma. The majority of troops in the Burma campaign were Indian Army who provided three Indian corps and eight infantry divisions, along with the two British infantry divisions, two West African and one East African Division. In numerical terms there were about 340,000 Indian troops, 100,000 British and 90,000 African troops.

The book also looks at American training pamphlets preparing troops for operations in the SWPA, where American forces were driven out of the Philippines; the US forces together with the Australian Army learnt from their experiences of fighting in the jungles of Malaya, New Guinea and the SWPA. They were also successful in defeating the Imperial Japanese Army in the jungle. This was achieved in the jungles through training, based on the doctrine of the training pamphlets, and experience as 'Bill' Slim wrote: 'training will tell you what the noise means, will enable you to make up by quickness and observation what your vision lacks in range and teach you to move steadily and quietly, and how to keep in touch'. (*A Note on Jungle Fighting in Burma*)

The army in Burma in 1942 was unprepared for jungle warfare, despite the fact that a large proportion of the country was covered by jungle, especially the eastern and western frontiers and the Arakan hills. In February 1941 the Governor of Burma was assured by the War Office that Burma did not require any more troops as it was highly improbable that Burma would ever become involved in war. In early 1942, the Japanese attacked Burma, firstly to protect the flanks of its conquests in Malaya and the Dutch East Indies (modern-day Indonesia). The airfields in Burma were within striking distance of both regions, and occupation denied the British and Americans strategic access. Secondly the Japanese wanted to control the Burma Road and thus cut off American supplies of military aid to the Chinese Nationalists.

After the political separation from India in 1937, the regular army in Burma consisted of four battalions of the Burma Rifles and two British battalions. The Burma Rifles were employed on garrison duties and saw very little action. Despite the Burmese tribesmen's familiarity with the jungle, Burma Rifles battalions participated in training and tactics for the open warfare of the plains rather than for jungle warfare. The two British battalions stationed in Burma in December 1941 were the 2nd Battalion the Gloucestershire Regiment and the 2nd Battalion the King's Own Yorkshire Light Infantry. They had undergone limited jungle training and were seriously ill-equipped. All that could be spared was two Bren guns per battalion, although the minimum request for each battalion was four Brens, two anti-tank rifles, two 2-inch mortars and two 3-inch mortars. The British units of all arms amounted to about 40,000 men. The garrison in Burma was reinforced by the Indian Army, namely 13th Indian Infantry Brigade in April and 16th Indian Infantry Brigade in November 1941 with 17th Indian Division, commanded by Acting Major General Jackie Smyth VC, also earmarked for Burma. The general standard of training of the Indian formations was low even before it was sent to Burma. This was largely due to the huge expansion of the Indian Army at the beginning of war where the army increased from 240,000 men in 1939 to 1.5 million in 1941. The result of this was that units were 'milked' of officers and NCOs to help form new units. Many of the newly formed infantry battalions had few regular officers and very little training. For example, Brigadier David 'Punch' Cowan, officiating as Director of Military Training in India, had agreed with Smyth that 17th Indian Division needed a further six weeks' training once it had arrived in Iraq, where it was originally destined. Two of its brigades, the 44th and 45th, were nevertheless sent to Malaya. Thus, all that was sent to Burma of the original division was one brigade, the 46th, and the Divisional HQ. Although it was strengthened by the attachment of 16th and 48th Indian Brigades, and 2nd Burma Brigade, the formation was not a fully integrated fighting force.

On 20 January 1942 the Japanese 15th Army, comprising 33rd and 55th Divisions, invaded Burma. These were trained and battle-hardened troops who had fought in China, not necessarily jungle-trained but lightly equipped for fighting in South East Asia. The IJA seized and maintained the initiative in the jungle, particularly as the Commonwealth troops were equipped with motor transport and therefore were tied to the roads and were continually out-flanked in the jungle. The Japanese also had command of the air.

The bridge at Sittang was of vital importance to both the Japanese and the Allies, since it was only a hundred miles from Rangoon, a vital supply link both for the Burma Road to China and for reinforcements and supplies for the Burma campaign. General Archibald Wavell, American British Dutch Australian (ABDA) Commander and Lieutenant General Hutton, Commander-in-Chief (C-in-C) Burma thought that it was best to keep as much distance between the enemy and Rangoon. Hutton's plan was to keep 17th Indian Division as a holding force east of Sittang so that reinforcements such as 7th Armoured Brigade could arrive to fight in the Pegu area as if this fell Rangoon would be quick to follow. As a result Smyth was refused permission to withdraw early to the bridge to build up a defensive position to the west, which was unfortunate since the ground was suitable for open warfare in which the 17th Indian Division had been trained. The plan was for all three brigades to cross the Sittang on 22 February, but due to the fog of war 16th and 46th Indian Infantry Brigades made little headway and 48th Indian Infantry Brigade only made a relatively short march westwards due to aerial bombing by Allied aircraft. On 23 February Brigadier Hugh Jones consulted with the battalion commanding officers holding the bridge and decided to request permission to blow up the bridge. He thought the 16th and 46th Brigades were too broken up to fight their way through the Japanese forces. Smyth gave his permission and the bridge was evacuated at 5am. Shortly afterwards Hugh Jones got a message that 16th Indian Infantry Brigade were planning to attack the bridge at first light. He broke down after hearing this news. It was a decision that continued to haunt him and eventually he drowned himself in 1952. Officers left on the other side of the bridge felt that senior commanders had panicked and demolished the bridge in haste. The Sittang Bridge disaster sealed the fate of the defending forces. Most battalions lost over half their strength whereas there were only 400 Japanese were killed and wounded in the battle. The 17th Division was left with just 80 officers, 69 Viceroy Commissioned officers (Indian officers who bridged the gap between British officers commanding Indian troops and non commissioned officers) and 3,335 other ranks – just 41% of its authorised strength – and was reduced to 1,420 rifles, 56 Bren guns and 68 Thompson sub-machine guns. Hutton was relieved of his command to be replaced by General Harold Alexander as C-in-C Burma. At the same time theatre command reverted from ABDA to General Headquarters (GHQ) India. Smyth went on extended sick leave to be replaced by Major General David 'Punch' Cowan who commanded the division until 1945 when it retook Rangoon. Together with the Fall of Singapore on 14 February, the two disasters were a huge blow to the prestige of the British Empire across South East Asia and particularly in India.

The defence of Rangoon was now unfeasible due to the lack of troops and equipment. The Army in Burma received further reinforcements, but they were badly trained, Although the battle-hardened and well-equipped, 7th Armoured Brigade arrived fresh from the Western Desert to shore up the defences, little alternative now remained other than retreating northwards to Mandalay. On 16 March, General W. J. Slim was appointed Corps Commander of Burcorps, and noted that his troops were ill-trained and ill-equipped for jungle warfare. The Army in Burma had no real chance of stopping the Japanese after Sittang Bridge and encountered a string of defeats. The British withdrew to India when it became clear that no other alternative remained. It was the longest retreat in British military history.

However the lessons of the retreat from Burma were closely studied in India. It was generally acknowledged that failure in Burma was due in large amount to the rapid expansion of the Indian, British and Burmese armies and a lack of often basic training but particularly in jungle warfare. Too much reliance had been placed on motor transport rather than the pack transport needed for jungle warfare. Although formations such as the 48th Indian Infantry Brigade under Brigadier Cameron performed admirably after experience in the jungle, particularly when his brigade adopted the tactic of 'all round defence' in the jungle. Tactical lessons learned in Burma included the importance of patrolling and junior leadership was seen as the key to success against the Japanese in the jungle. The most detailed investigation was produced soon after arrival in the Imphal plain when Cowan instructed Brigadier Cameron and a committee of battalion commanders to identify new training, tactics and equipment needed to fight successfully in Burma. The committee realised that training in jungle was of vital importance. Various weapons were targeted as essential for jungle fighting, such as the *dhah*, an Indian knife, for clearing jungle undergrowth. It was realised that weapons had to be kept clean due to the problems of jamming in the moist jungle atmosphere which hastened rust and corrosion. The report also highlighted the value of the 2-inch mortar and the range of the 3-inch mortar, although the latter was less portable. Tanks were viewed as good for morale and effective for use in close support of the infantry. Finally, all arms of combat were to be jungle trained.

All the lessons from Burma were eventually encapsulated into the third edition of the pamphlet *Military Training Pamphlet* (MTP) No. 9 (India) entitled *Jungle Warfare* published in August 1942. It was considerably larger than the first edition, with an increase from eleven to seventy-three pages, and now had a distribution of 45,000 copies to all the officers of the Indian and British Armies and NCOs of the British Army in India. It stressed that the Japanese were not 'supermen' and that better-trained Allied troops, whether British, Australian, Indian or Gurkha, had proved this more than once. The new edition included a section on Japanese tactical methods which were described at length but were summed up in the four words: mobility, speed, infiltration and encirclement. Other sections were on attack and defence for all arms against Japanese tactics, ambushes, patrols, administrative problems, minor tactics and training. For attack, encircling and filleting were the two suggested methods and aggressive patrols and ambushes were to be used in both attack and defence. It was realised that as the jungle was alien to nearly all the fighting troops they needed practical training in it. Training was divided into four areas of jungle craft: map reading and the use of the compass to find one's way in the jungle; concealment; jungle lore; and use of weapons to achieve the maximum effect. The training manual was a very important milestone in the development of the Indian Army learning to adapt to jungle warfare in Burma. When 5th Indian Division were transferred from the Middle East to India for the Burma campaign they used this edition for their training, calling it their 'bible'.

The retreat from Burma was followed by the equally unsuccessful First Arakan campaign of September 1942–March 1943, and the ensuing Japanese counteroffensive was yet again a defeat inflicted on the British and Indian troops by a numerically inferior force. It was the first time that British and Indian forces came up against the defensive bunkers of the Imperial Japanese Army. The campaign had again been a tactical failure. Repeated attacks on a narrow front against the bunkers had proved disastrous at an early stage, and the encircling tactics employed by the Japanese at the end of the campaign had again proved decisive. The outstanding failure in the campaign noted by most reports was the overall low level of training and the very low standard of training of reinforcements.

After these disastrous campaigns, GHQ India made some important changes in senior staff officers and front-line commanders to improve military effectiveness. Most significantly Wavell was appointed Viceroy of India and was replaced by General Claude Auchinleck as C-in-C India in

June 1943. Operational control for campaigns was now to be conducted by the newly appointed Supreme Allied Commander in South East Asia, Lord Louis Mountbatten. A change in front-line leadership was also made. Lieutenant-General Sir George Giffard took over Eastern Army, a veteran of the bush fighting in East Africa during the First World War. Later that year General Slim was appointed as Fourteenth Army Commander and a range of experienced divisional commanders were also appointed, such as Major Generals Frank Messery and 'Pete' Rees, commanding 7th and 19th Indian Divisions respectively, both of whom had not fared well in North Africa but became very distinguished commanders in the Burma campaign. At the same time changes were made in the training structure as Major General Reginald Savory, who had commanded 23rd Indian Division in Assam, was made Inspector of Infantry. The appointments of Savory, Auchinleck and Slim were an important factor in the eventual defeat of the Japanese as for the first time the key figures in Indian military affairs were all drawn from the Indian Army and understood the traditions and ways of the Indian Army.

Wavell convened the Infantry Committee in June 1943 with a brief to improve the standard of British and Indian infantry in theatre. The Committee studied the problem for two weeks. It blamed the defeats in Burma and the Arakan on the 'milking' and expansion of the Indian Army, the failure to recognise the importance of infantry in battle, the lack of basic training and experienced leadership, the fighting on two fronts, the lack of collective training as formations, prolonged periods of contact with the enemy, the problems of providing trained reinforcements, the problem of malaria and the lack of resources. The Committee's proposed solution was thorough basic training of recruits, followed by a period of jungle training for both British and Indian troops under designated training divisions and the need for a definitive jungle warfare doctrine was also highlighted. The 14th and 39th Indian Divisions were chosen as the training divisions. British infantry reinforcements were trained in jungle warfare by 52nd Brigade. The training divisions made an important contribution to teaching individual jungle skills, shown by the example of the Punjab Regiment, in which 1,957 trained soldiers from the training divisions joined the regiment's battalions.

Auchinleck ensured that jungle warfare training formed the main focus of all training carried out by units, formations and at training establishments throughout India. The work of specialised training establishments already dealing with jungle fighting was stepped up. The Jungle Warfare School at Comilla moved to Sevoke in 1943. Each course lasted for fifteen days and demonstrated new tactics required for jungle warfare. Lessons learnt at the school were then taken back to the battalion by officers who acted as instructors and ensured these ideas were put into practice. Due to the demand for places on the course a second jungle warfare school was opened at Shimoga. Collective training in Fourteenth Army was also carried out. For example, 7th Indian Division moved to the Chhindwara area in January 1943 and was one of the first formations to embark on jungle training. The Division went on to fight successfully in the second battle of the Arakan and the battles for Kohima and Imphal.

In conclusion, GHQ India, the training divisions, the jungle warfare schools, training within Fourteenth Army's divisions and the new doctrine of jungle warfare encapsulated in *The Jungle Book* provided a basis for uniformly jungle trained troops ready to defeat the terrain, the climate, the diseases and the Japanese.

A similar process occurred in the Australian and American armed forces that ultimately proved successful in the campaigns in New Guinea and SWPA as well as the American and Chinese troops fighting in northern Burma under the command of General Joseph Stilwell. The New Guinea campaign is often overshadowed by the Marine operations in the Pacific and the subsequent liberation of the Philippines, however General Douglas MacArthur commanded 1,377,000 American, Australian and Dutch troops, who proved adept in fighting in the jungle. The jungle warfare experience was shared across the Allied nations. Colonel Forster on the British Army staff in Washington was made responsible for gathering information about jungle warfare equipment and the resulting information was distributed to GHQ India, the War Office and Australia Command. In August 1943 the first of many jungle warfare liaison letters were passed between GHQ India and Australia Command with the War Office, New Zealand and US Commands later included in the circulation.

CHAPTER I

DOCTRINE

The campaigns in Malaya, Burma and First Arakan had showed that *MTP No. 9 Jungle Warfare* (third edition) was an inadequate basis for training as the manuals did not fully address new tactical problems such as bunkers. It was apparent that many officers had not read the training manuals or carried out training according to their guidelines. Thus in September 1943, the Military Training Directorate finally produced a comprehensive jungle warfare doctrine with the publication of 80,000 copies of the fourth edition of *MTP No. 9 (India): The Jungle Book*. The new edition had doubled the circulation of the previous editions of *MTP No. 9* that passed on the latest knowledge on jungle fighting to every officer and all British NCOs. Its clearly stated purpose was to help commanding officers train their units in the specialised fighting methods needed to beat the IJA in the jungle, stating: 'In principle there is nothing new in jungle warfare, but the environment of the jungle is new to many of our troops. Special training is therefore necessary to accustom them to jungle conditions and to teach them jungle methods', listing the examples of jungle craft, physical fitness, good marksmanship and decentralised control as the necessary attributes that needed addressing in jungle warfare training. It had a new format, including photographs and cartoons for the first time, which was in stark contrast to the usual dull training manuals and was intended to popularise training.

The training manual assimilated all the lessons from the previous editions of *MTP No. 9* and included lessons from the First Arakan and from American and Australian experiences of fighting the Japanese in the Pacific. In the section on the infantry, it reiterated the importance of this arm as the most important in the jungle. It noted the need for thorough training in the use of rifles, bayonets, grenades, automatic weapons and mortars in the jungle and the importance of fire control. The major change in the contents of this pamphlet was a section suggesting how to counter the style of Japanese defence such as encountered in the Arakan. For instance for the infantry, it suggested the employment of previously underused anti-tank weapons. Co-operation with the other arms was also essential in bunker busting. The artillery could provide barrage fire on a narrow front and it was suggested that lifts of a hundred yards every three minutes were needed in average jungle and a slower rate in thicker jungle. It noted that aircraft and tanks could be of equal value in support of infantry, particularly against bunkers. As in previous editions of *MTP* No. 9, there were sections on attack, active defence and ambushes. The section on patrolling had increased, while the chapter on withdrawal had been reduced to an emphatic: 'THERE WILL BE NO WITHDRAWAL'. There were also detailed sections on maintenance, detailing for example the scale of rations needed and supply details. The appendices had sections on jungle craft, living in the country and first aid in the jungle. The pamphlet covered all the lessons that had been learnt since 1941 and as a result the individual sections were very thorough. The manual was used by the Indian Army for the remainder of the Second World War. It was by no means perfect, however, and was meant to be added to and improved upon. Indeed, *The Jungle Book* later formed the basis for two War Office manuals in 1944–45 – *MTP No. 51: Preparation for Warfare in the Far East* and *MTP No. 52: Warfare in the Far East* – demonstrating that it was the Indian Army rather than the British Army who pioneered jungle warfare doctrine. *The Jungle Book* together with the other ancillary training manuals became the focus for the dissemination of doctrine in India for all the units and formations preparing for the war in Burma.

FM 72-20: Jungle Warfare, the definitive American manual for jungle doctrine, was issued by the War Department in 1944. It superseded and expanded upon the *Basic Field Manual: Jungle Warfare* which had been issued in 1941 and revised ever since, and consolidated the lessons learned in the Pacific.

Military Training Pamphlet No. 9 (India)
The Jungle Book

I. PREFACE.

1. This pamphlet is written to assist commanders in training their units to fight the Japanese in jungles. It contains much of the available information which has been gained from experience in recent operations in South Eastern Asia, and it gives lessons which have been learned sometimes at a great price. It should be read in conjunction with the pamphlet "Japanese in Battle—Enemy Methods" and can be regarded as being Part II of that pamphlet.

2. In principle there is nothing new in jungle warfare, but the environment of the jungle is new to many of our troops. Special training is therefore necessary to accustom them to jungle conditions and to teach them jungle methods.

3. Woodcraft, silent movement, concealment, deception, keen eyesight and hearing, and above all good marksmanship and superb physical fitness are the requisites of jungle fighting.

4. Experience shows that command must be decentralized so that junior leaders will be confronted with situations in which they must make decisions and act without delay on their own responsibility. The ability to make sound decisions can only follow from thorough training and continuous practice.

5. Since both jungle fighting and night fighting are characterized by limited vision and difficulties of maintaining control and direction, they have much in common with each other. If, therefore, units are unable to train under jungle conditions, a high standard of night training must be achieved and will prove to be an excellent preparation for jungle fighting.

II. TOPOGRAPHY.

1. Jungle country varies from forests to mountainous jungle and the more open coastal and cultivated areas. Examples of various types of country in Burma are shown in photographs in Chapter II of the pamphlet "Japanese in Battle, Part I, Enemy Methods." A brief description of countries in South East Asia is given in Appendices A to F.

2. The features common to all jungle areas are scarcity of tracks, limited visibility for both air and ground forces, and difficulties of cross-country movement by all vehicles.

3. In general, there are three types of jungle: primary, secondary and coastal. Primary jungle is natural vegetation which has never been touched and

has remained in its original state. Visibility is limited to 20 or 30 yards, varying according to the slope of the ground and amount of foliage present. On the tops of hills the foliage is thin and in valleys it is extremely dense. Where there is a stream which has become blocked a swamp is often formed and this is sometimes passable; but these swamps generally extend only for a few hundred yards and can always be circumvented. Tracks exist, but they are seldom shown on maps. The jungle is never impassable to infantry at any place, though a dah, kukri or machete is necessary to cut new tracks or to remove undergrowth. The smaller the party, the more rapid the advance.

4. Secondary jungle occurs where the primary jungle has been cleared and allowed to grow up again. The vegetation usually takes the form of very dense ferns and brambles through which it is impossible to force a way without some form of cutting instrument.

5. Along the coastal areas, the jungle often becomes more open, and consists of mangrove swamps and clearing of Kunai grass. Kunai grass grows to a height of four to eight feet, which precludes ground observation. In addition, there are coconut groves near inhabited areas.

6. Rivers in low country are generally broad and sluggish, but in the hills are deep and swift. They are no obstacle to determined, ingenious troops.

7. Paddy fields are very difficult going in the rainy season, but, although a man may sink knee-deep in mud, they are no real obstacle to hardy troops. In the dry season, except for the little "bands", they are good going, but are hard on all vehicles, even though tracked.

8. Rubber plantations vary according to their age; when young, they give cover similar to a field of potatoes. When mature, the symmetrical lines allow up to 200 yards ground visibility and give fair cover from the air.

9. Full-grown tea bushes give good cover for men but are never big enough to hide vehicles, guns or animals.

10. Jungle almost invariably means great humidity and high rainfall, also many streams and swamps, with attendant disadvantages and discomforts such as mosquitoes and malaria, leeches, chills, etc.

11. The constant object must be to exploit the special features of the country to our advantage by developing tactics suited to the particular conditions; and, by training and knowledge of jungle craft to minimise the physical discomforts.

III. JUNGLE CRAFT.

1. The term jungle craft implies the ability of a soldier to live and fight in the jungle; to be able to move from point to point and arrive at his objective fit to fight; to use ground and vegetation to the best advantage; and be able to "melt" into the jungle either by freezing or intelligent use of camouflage; to recognise and be able to use native foods; and possess the ability to erect rapidly temporary shelters to ward off tropical downpours. A jungle soldier should be sufficiently well versed in jungle lore to recognise instantly the cry or call of disturbed birds. His ear should be attuned to normal jungle noises in order that he may detect foreign or man-made sounds. He must learn to rely on his observation of broken twigs and branches, of trampled undergrowth and of disturbed mould, to detect the recent presence or proximity of humans. He must use his sense of smell (it is a curious fact, but the Jap soldier possesses a peculiar, unpleasant odour which is most persistent). He must readily recognise the danger of tracks converging at either watering places or gardens, and approach such areas with caution. He must learn to move through the jungle in darkness and be able to retrace his steps. He must learn to move silently, to avoid stepping on rotting logs and twigs and otherwise giving away his presence to the enemy. In short, the jungle is the home of the jungle soldier, and the sooner he learns to feel at home there the better.

2. Further notes in connection with jungle craft are included in Appendix "G".

IV. GENERAL TACTICS.

1. In the succeeding paragraphs, the conditions envisaged are those of jungle in which the outstanding characteristic is LACK OF VISIBILITY.

2. It will help to understand the principles of operations in this type of country if they are thought of as night operations; the same difficulty in keeping direction; the same difficulty of using covering fire; the same reliance upon the ear rather than they eye, and the consequent need for absolute silence.

3. Night operations are normally undertaken to surprise the enemy by making use of poor visibility to obtain cover from view. In jungle fighting similar conditions prevail and the jungle must therefore be regarded as a friendly cloak, which enables infantry to close unobserved with the enemy and, therefore, the more easily to kill him.

4. Since jungle so favours the attacker, a purely passive defence in the jungle is doomed to disaster and must not be tolerated.

5. Defensive measures will, however, be necessary for consolidation, when at rest to deny an area to the enemy or to provide a firm base for further offensive operations.

6. The measures adopted will vary according to the task and circumstances of the force. Where a force is dependent upon a land L of C, it will be necessary to protect the L of C by a series of defended perimeters, which will act as the firm bases from which counter offensive and counter attack troops will operate and within which other troops may rest, transport may harbour and reserves of supplies, petrol and ammunition may be built up and maintained.

In the case of detached forces operating for a short period and carrying their own supplies, or for long periods and supplied by air, the necessity for the protection of the L of C is of little importance. In this case defence may well take the form of concealment away from tracks in dense jungle surrounded by patrols prepared to ambush any enemy who may approach; and by seldom staying in the same place too long.

7. In either case the main strength of the defence will lie with the offensive action of counter offensive troops, fighting patrols and ambushes rather than with the fire power of the static portion of the defence, though this is necessary for the close protection of the defended area.

8. When jungle is dense, rapid movement is necessarily confined to such jungle trails, game tracks and dry water courses as exist. These are few and normally are used by the Japanese when approaching. Frequent opportunities will, therefore, present themselves for ambushing the enemy, and all troops must be trained not only to lay the carefully designed and prepared ambush but also by means of a battle drill hastily to occupy an ambush position at short notice, as soon as they are aware of the approach of the enemy.

9. The formations to be adopted for the approach march, when within reach of the enemy, will be dictated by two main factors; the need for speed and the denseness of the jungle.

(a) When the need for speed in the actual advance is paramount, e.g., in order to forestall the enemy by seizing a tactical feature, troops will normally move along tracks, and the denser the jungle the more imperative does this become.

(b) When, on the other hand, speed in the advance is not paramount, it will be advantageous to advance on the broadest front which the denseness of the jungle and the required speed of advance permit. By this means, as soon as contact with the enemy is gained, his flanks and weak points can rapidly be located and a front or outflanking attack can be speedily launched without the delays which are otherwise imposed by having to deploy off the trail. In an encounter battle of this kind rapid and resolute action is necessary. This is likely to take one of two forms; either a front attack supported by all available weapons, which blasts its way forward on a narrow front astride the trail; or alternatively, and probably more frequently, the fixing of the enemy in front, whilst other troops outflank him on one or both flanks and attack him in the flank or rear. In either case the flank protection of the attacking force must never be neglected owing to the Japanese method of defence which frequently retains counter attack troops wide on the flank of their defensive positions.

10. Under certain conditions a third method may be necessary in order to reduce delay to the main body. This method seeks to isolate the enemy by fixing him in front, outflanking him on both sides and closing his escape in rear, whilst the main body by-passes his position and continues the advance. The enemy thus isolated can be destroyed in detail at leisure.

11. The diligence of the Japanese in the preparation of field works and their habit of placing their flanks on serious obstacles may under certain circumstances necessitate a direct attack.

12. Under these conditions the most detailed preliminary reconnaissance is essential to locate the strong points; the most intense fire support, which M. Gs., mortars, artillery and air bombardment can provide and ammunition supply will permit, must be arranged; and rehearsals of the attack should be carried out beforehand. Frontages should be small and objectives must be limited. The strong points should be reduced, like pill boxes, by special assault parties of infantry and pioneers or engineers with explosives; special mopping up parties must be detailed to ensure that all the Japanese in the area are destroyed. To assist in the destruction of pill boxes and "bunkers" every available weapon should be employed. A. Tk weapons, flame throwers and "beehives" have all proved their value.

13. In all jungle operations the problems of administration will have a tyrannical influence on the battle. For this reason, if tactical mobility is to be secured and tactical superiority over the enemy maintained, provision must be made not only for a considerable weight of direct air support but also for air supply to relieve the burden on the L of C. Owing to the difficulties of the country and the dissimilarity to other theatres considerable training, not only by ground formations and units but also by air squadrons and pilots, and the closest co-operation between the two, is necessary in order that the air effort may be applied economically and to the best advantage.

V. NOTES ON THE VARIOUS ARMS.

INFANTRY.

1. **General**.—Infantry is the paramount arm in jungles owing to its comparative mobility, and well trained infantry can dominate the jungle. Special training, however, is necessary to accustom troops to the jungle conditions and jungle life. This training must inculcate the ability to move quickly and silently; to find the way accurately and with confidence; to shoot straight and quickly at disappearing targets from all positions on the ground, out of trees and from the hip; to carry out tactical operations in the jungle by means of battle drills, known to all, and without waiting for detailed orders. Above all the highest pitch of physical toughness is essential in all ranks, particularly officers, and the leadership of junior commanders must be confident, offensive and inspiring.

2. **The rifle and bayonet**.—The jungle, the rifle and the bayonet are the infantryman's primary weapons. It is with these that he will attain final victory. His skill with them therefore must be supreme.

The feeling of loneliness and the bad visibility in the jungle tend to make men jumpy if they have not complete confidence in themselves. The highest standard of sub-unit and individual fire control is therefore necessary, and training must be directed to this end.

Against the Japanese, the mere threat of the bayonet is not sufficient. It must be used to kill them. It should be the ambition of every infantryman to redden his bayonet with the enemy's blood.

3. **Automatic weapons.**—The general principles for the employment of automatic weapons are:—

(a) Normally use single shot fire, save ammunition and don't disclose the location of your automatic weapon.

(b) NEVER use automatic fire, unless you have a really worth-while target, or in the final stages of the assault.

(c) Once you have disclosed your position by the use of automatic fire, take the first opportunity of moving to an alternative position to the flank or forward.

4. **Mortars.**—Owing to their greater mobility, mortars will frequently have to replace artillery in support of the infantry. They must be used boldly in order to reduce the distance to the O.P.

A high standard of training is necessary in observation of fire, in application of fire and in rapidly coming into action. The problem of the maintenance of ammunition supply will often make the employment of carrying parties necessary. Infantry so employed will rarely be wasted.

5. **Anti-tank weapons.**—Anti-tank weapons of all sorts, rifles, guns and grenades, apart from their normal employment, can be usefully used at short range against pill boxes and "bunkers" to destroy them.

6. **Grenades.**—Owing to the close nature of jungle fighting grenades have an enhanced value and at least one should be carried by most men. In defence the grenade has an advantage over all other weapons in that its silent delivery does not disclose its point of origin and thereby give away the position of the thrower.

7. **Carriers.**—Carriers are particularly vulnerable in jungle and must NEVER be employed in a tank role. If used in a forward role they must be closely accompanied and protected by infantry.

They will frequently be most effectively employed to carry forward ammunition, water, cable, etc., to the forward troops and to assist the porterage of heavy weapons over difficult or vulnerable routes to their position.

ARTILLERY

1. **General.**—In jungle areas there are certain difficulties as regards observation, communications, movement and battery positions, but in the case, for example, of anti-tank work, the artillery problem is simplified.

The principle of the concentration of artillery fire is as sound in jungle as it has been proved to be in North Africa.

The principle that the infantry must always have close support, no matter what type of country is encountered must be borne in mind. It is for this reason that the divisional artillery is allotted a proportion of mortar batteries which can be carried over any country the infantry can negotiate. It is not sufficient for F.O.Os. to accompany an outflanking attack, trusting on wireless to get through to the gun; a proportion of artillery weapons must go too to give that close and guaranteed support to which infantry are entitled.

Wherever reference is made to "guns" in the ensuing paragraphs, it should be taken to include any weapon with which field or mountain artillery is equipped, i.e., 25 prs. 3.7" hows. or mortars.

2. **Physical fitness.**—The standard of physical fitness must be very high. Guns may have to be man-handled over long distances, and personnel must be prepared to fight with the barest minimum of M.T. and to be self-contained for periods up to 48 hours. This particularly applies to O.P. parties who may have to walk into action carrying their wireless equipment. The tendency

has been to be too roadbound; real determination to get anywhere with the essential vehicles will seldom fail.

3. **Improvisation.**—The situation frequently varies at great speed and unit must, therefore, be prepared for anything. At some time or other, improvisation will certainly be necessary to overcome unexpected difficulties. Although a drill for manoeuvre, deployment, etc., is required, a rigid drill may break down; for example, when a proportion of unit vehicles are destroyed. Unfavourable circumstances must therefore be introduced during exercise to train officers and men to develop their powers of initiative and resource, and to meet unusual conditions no matter how impossible they may appear. Local resources must be used when possible to save man-handling or to economise in vehicles.

4. **Speed.**—Operations in the jungle against the Japanese have proved that artillery support to be effective must often be provided rapidly. Information of enemy movement is frequently scanty; contact may occur at any time or place and actions may consequently develop very quickly with no preliminary warning. The following points must therefore be kept in mind:—

(a) The necessity for close liaison with the troops whom the guns are supporting. F.O.Os. must be well forward and in close touch with battalion or company commanders, and must be prepared to make and carry out immediate fire plans, without reference to their battery commanders.

(b) Communication between O.Ps. and guns must be guaranteed, and at least a proportion of the guns must always be able to give support under all conditions. The shorter the communications, the better they will be.

(c) Speed into action and the reduction of the time between orders for action and first round must be continually practised. It is NOT necessary to record zero lines before getting off the first round.

(d) Fire plans must be simple. There is no time for complicated fire plans in this type of warfare.

5. **Selection of gun positions.**—(a) Except in dense jungle, suitable positions for mortars and 3.7" hows. may be found in clearings. Mortar batteries may provide support in the initial stages of an attack and may be strengthened by the 3.7" how. batteries when they can be got into action.

(b) 25 prs. will be used when the opposition is heavy; their movement will be largely confined to roads and tracks. In thick country, positions may be difficult to find except near roads. The immediate vicinity of straight and open roads and tracks should, however, be avoided if possible owing to the danger of low level air attack.

(c) Reconnaissance parties of 25 pr. batteries and regiments should move well ahead of the guns to find suitable O.P. and gun areas.

(d) All types of artillery must be prepared to fire in any direction and positions must be sited accordingly.

6. **Gunnery.**—In thick jungle, shell bursts will be difficult to observe and, therefore, full use must be made of any means of simplifying this problem. Smoke shell, air burst, H.E. and shrapnel (if available) can all be used; the opening range can be estimated by using methods such as traverse.

Ranging by sound can also be employed and is quite simple provided that the normal rules of ranging are used and bold corrections are given.

Air photos are of considerable value for spotting targets, helping map reading and getting opening rounds near the target.

7. **Artillery in the attack.**—(a) Attacks in jungle country are usually made on narrow fronts and are supported by quick or standard barrages or by concentrations. The guns available may be only one battery or one regiment; training is required in putting down barrages quickly after registration of one point only.

(b) Experience has shown that the Jap digs himself into deep "fox-holes" against which intense artillery fire is needed to be effective. Barrage frontages must therefore be very narrow and areas allotted for concentrations must be small. In thick country the rate of advance of barrages must be very slow to conform to the rate of the infantry advance. Infantry must keep as close to the barrage or concentration as possible. Barrages may have to pause at intervals while mopping-up takes place.

(c) If heavily attacked the Jap will sometimes withdraw into the jungle and later counter attack, sometimes within 10 to 15 minutes of the capture of the position. Before an attack starts, it may often be possible to register likely forming up places for such enemy counter attacks. Alternatively, registration of areas flanking a position must be carried out immediately the position is captured.

(d) Artillery may be called on to support an immediate counter attack against enemy who have infiltrated into an area. A creeping barrage may be the best form of support. An F.O.O. must already be with the infantry commander and fully in touch with the situation. Extreme accuracy on the opening line is not necessary; the object will be to bring down fire in the minimum of time, to dwell there until the infantry arrive, and then for both shells and infantry to move forward at as fast a pace as conditions permit. A battery in action should be able to put down such a barrage within 15 minutes of being asked to do so.

8. Artillery in Defence.—(a) In thickly enclosed country where control hinges on a central road, defence is often based on areas in depth along the road. Artillery will normally be sited within such areas and must be prepared for all round fire.

(b) Methods of calling for and bringing down fire in support of adjacent areas must be practised. In order to get observation it will frequently be necessary to have observing officers with companies in addition to an officer at battalion headquarters.

(c) Mortar smoke bombs can be of great value for indicating targets to artillery. They will be of even greater value for this purpose if coloured smoke can be provided.

9. Anti-Tank Artillery.—In jungle, tanks are usually confined to roads or tracks. Guns must be sited under cover off the road ready to fire on the sides and rear of tanks as they pass down the road. The field of fire may often consist of a narrow lane cut through the jungle to a distance of only 40 yards from the road.

10. Light A. A. Artillery.—(a) The whole length of a jungle road may form a defile. Columns may have to be protected by light A. A. guns disposed along the column and firing on the move, or from wheels if the column halts.

(b) A proportion of the light A. A. guns will normally be detailed to protect first artillery positions in clearings. The occupation of such positions by a mixed gun group requires the closest liaison and must be practised.

11. Artillery communication.—The usual method of communication will be L/T. Lines must be carefully laid and are best secured by lifting them on to trees above vehicle height. Long communications are difficult to maintain and must be avoided.

In jungle country wireless range is appreciably reduced and it sometimes fails at night. A different frequency may be required for use after dark.

All types of W.T. sets will have to be carried on occasions and practice in this, and in maintaining communication by means of wireless alone, is necessary.

Liaison officers are very useful. On many occasions they are the only means of controlling movement and getting in touch with units rapidly. Both liaison officers and despatch riders may often have to work in pairs, one covering the other.

ENGINEERS

1. Jungle conditions do not necessarily imply a new engineer role nor do they alter the general principles of engineer work and organization. They do affect very materially methods of execution. These have to be adapted to the new environment. This is the point that must be kept constantly in view during training.

2. In the jungle large concentrations of resources and their rapid movement will usually be impracticable. Engineer tasks therefore will have to be done not only with reduced resources but also with less possibilities of switching these resources from one job to another. The general effect will be to restrict engineering to its less elaborate forms and to necessitate the utmost use of what the jungle itself contains. Engineers must be taught how to find and how to use the jungle products, particularly its timber and "tie tie".

3. Because of the paucity and low capacity of the communications it will probably be found that the engineer component of a force will have to be a task detachment, i.e., equipped for a particular piece of work. This organization on a task basis makes engineer intelligence and reconnaissance more than ever important. It will have to be well forward in space and time. Naturally the period for which a task force will remain suitable will be limited. It must therefore be backed by a front to rear organization permitting reinforcement, maintenance, reallocation of equipment and leap frogging.

4. Since our policy is an offensive one, the object in most operations will be to get on. Engineer training should concentrate on the means to this end. In most cases it will be matter of making and improving communications. Road making and bridging will take the bulk of the engineer effort. Consequently the technique of execution of these in the jungle should be one of the first subjects for training. Engineers must be experts in the making of jeep tracks and in their subsequent development to take 15 cwt. and other vehicles; they must be ready also to ensure the quick passage of waterways and to develop crossings capable of carrying the heaviest loads with the force.

5. Next in importance will be the overcoming of enemy attempts to delay the advance. This will mean engineer detachments well forward and these must be experts in the recognition and rapid removal of enemy mines and other delaying devices. Speed will be the dominant factor in their work and must be emphasized in all training. It can only be obtained through practice and by learning the devices and methods used by the enemy.

6. Where prepared positions have to be attacked, there will be calls on the engineers to deal with strong points. These will have to be met rapidly which means battle drill. This battle drill must be learnt with the other arms engaged. This last is essential. Assault training by one arm alone is valueless.

7. In all this work there is increased need for engineers to be air-minded. They must be trained to look out for well drained sites likely to make landing grounds. They must be able to select and prepare dropping places. They must take full advantage of the air to assist in the reconnaissance of roads and bridging sites and they must be able to read air photos to this end. They must be ready to use the air to get engineer stores forward. This last matter means that the technique of stores dropping should be practised, and engineer commanders must be ready to send equipped detachments by air.

AIRCRAFT

1. **General.**—The general rules governing army-air co-operation apply also to jungle warfare. They may be found in MTP No. 8 (India). Methods will differ to some extent owing to the nature of the country which makes it difficult for pilots either to reconnoitre for the Army or to identify targets which they are called upon to attack. It is therefore all the more necessary that the personal touch between commanders of the two Services should be close, and in particular that both pilots in the air and front line commanders on the ground should appreciate each other's problems. Visits by pilots to units in contact with the enemy are of the greatest value, both to themselves for learning the Army problem, and to the troops for learning how they can best help the Air Force.

Owing to the dense nature of the country it is almost impossible for pilots to assess the value of their attacks; those which are being of the greatest help to the troops may appear to the pilots to be a waste of effort against a featureless patch of jungle. Forward commanders should therefore quick to pass on information concerning the assistance obtained from air attacks.

2. **Reconnaissance.**—Though visual reconnaissance and pin pointing are difficult, a high standard can be reached by an experienced pilot. The pilot can however be helped by reducing to the minimum the number of tasks he is required to perform on each sortie. The less he is given to do in the air the more information he will probably bring back. Reconnaissance is usually done at a very low level and this is a heavy strain on the pilot.

3. **Photography.**—This is of two kinds. This first is the photo taken by the pilot to supplement his visual impression when he thinks he has seen something worth further study, and the second is the regular cover of certain areas for intelligence purposes and for the use of commanders in planning attacks. In making demands for the latter, commanders should remember that the organization of flying, processing and production of prints, their distribution and interpretation, take time. They should therefore look well ahead for their photo requirements and make their demands early. The value of air photography for every purpose is far greater than was at one time expected, particularly for artillery and engineer plans. The fullest advantage should be taken of air photos, which will frequently disclose information denied to the eyes of the pilot by reason of the speed of his machine combined with the closeness of the country.

4. **Recognition and Identification (Contact/R.).**—It will usually be impossible for forward troops to indicate their position to friendly aircraft. It may on occasions however be possible to indicate to the pilot the position of company headquarters, by means of coloured umbrellas, strips or some other device, supplemented if necessary by flares to draw attention. It is necessary to experiment and to improvise; systems will improve with practice, and when a good one is found it should be made known. It is in problems such as this that friendly discussion is of particular value between pilots and the troops they support. The system devised must be practised until it becomes a drill by both pilots and troops on the ground.

5. **Indication of Targets.**—If a pilot knows exactly what he has to hit, and can identify it, he can concentrate all his energies to that end and will not have to be thinking all the time of safety precautions. There is a great advantage therefore in indicating the target to him by visual means. This can be done either by firing smoke at the target, or by so placing smoke that it indicates the position of the target when the target itself is out of range of our guns or mortars. It has often been found that the simplest method of guiding attacking aircraft to their targets is to have the attack led by a Tac/R pilot. These pilots by their close personal contact with the formation they support and by their visits to forward troops, usually know their area a great deal better than other pilots.

6. **Army Air Support Controls.**—The difficulty of bringing up sufficient artillery in jungle country, and of keeping it supplied with ammunition, makes direct support from the air of even greater importance than in other theatres.

The tentacle is the forward terminal of a communication system exclusively for the transmission of air support demands and of intelligence connected with

THE ADVANCE.

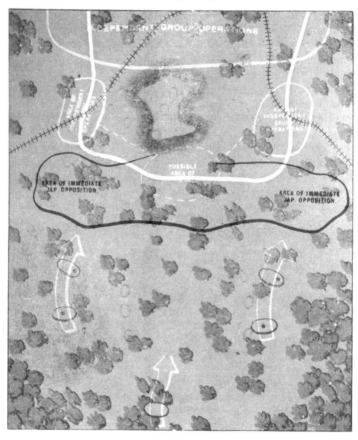

AIR DROPPING POINT ●
AIR AERODROME

DEFENDED AREA ⬭

air operations. If information is not passed back on this channel the Army will not get the best air support available. At Air Force formation and unit H.Qs. the thirst for information from forward units is insatiable. Commanders must therefore regard the tentacle as one of their most important possessions and must make full use of it. It should not be used, except in extreme emergency, for any but army/air matters.

7. **Supply by Air**.—The ability of a force to be supplied by air not only confers on it a freedom of manoeuvre which is otherwise denied it by reason of its dependence on an L of C, but also relieves that L of C of a burden, which in areas ill-provided with communications is bound to be heavy. Training of army formations and pilots of aircraft is essential, if satisfactory results are to be obtained and losses of supplies to be reduced to the minimum. Formations must be trained in the methods of providing landmarks, of marking out dropping zones, of rapidly collecting and distributing dropped supplies and of the salvage of parachutes and containers. Whilst open spaces make the best dropping zones, they are NOT essential to successful air dropping.

VI. THE ADVANCE TO CONTACT.

1. The advance through the jungle usually consists of movement on narrow jungle tracks or native trails. The latter may be only 18 inches to 2 feet wide, and the former no more than 4 to 6 feet wide. In certain regions, both are liable to deteriorate rapidly, even under foot traffic. Roads may be available in some areas but, unless all-weather, are liable to deteriorate with heavy use. A special feature of the advance by jungle tracks and trails is that every item of equipment may often have to be carried on the man or by porter transport.

2. Whenever possible the advance should be made by separate columns in approach march formation along all suitable lines of approach. This affords

(Opposite:)
1. Independent Groups may be allotted to support the movement of columns by operations against enemy rear areas. Additional units may also operate even farther in depth on a larger scale.
2. Columns move forward through successive defended areas with direct Air support and reconnaissance.
3. Air dropping points are selected for each defended area. Supply dropping by R.A.F. will supplement ground supply to assure constant supply in the event of the ground L of C being cut.

ADVANCE ON A BROAD FRONT.

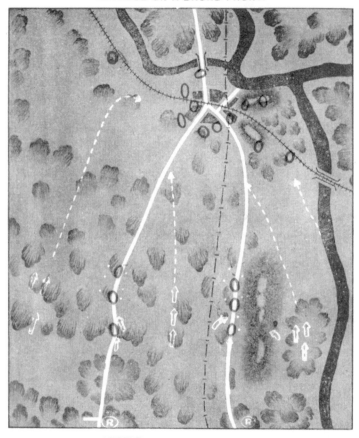

LEGEND

Blue	Enemy troops
Red	Own troops
(R)	Reserve on track

opportunities for rapidly outflanking the enemy, while preventing any similar attempt by the enemy. Air photos will be invaluable for determining the location of tracks and the possible routes of advance, and these photos may be of special value to forward commanders.

3. Reconnaissance by all units cannot be stressed too greatly. Lightly equipped patrols well forward will be responsible for local reconnaissance. Where the ground permits, these patrols should be mounted or carried in jeeps.

4. The advance may often become a race for successive tactical objectives. Speed is, therefore, of great importance. Generally each column will advance on a narrow front. In a rapid advance in thick country it may not be possible to secure the flanks since flank patrols may have to cut their way through thick vegetation and be unable to keep up with troops moving on the tracks. In such cases security may have to be limited to strong detachments to the front, with piquets placed on transverse tracks. Flank protection must, however, be provided when passing through cleared areas.

5. When halted, every body of troops will secure itself from attack from any direction by means of an all round defence.

6. Every operation under jungle conditions is made with limited information, and even this information is difficult to obtain. Commanders must realise that reconnaissances which consist merely of moving from one blind spot to another can frequently be a waste of time.

7. Reliance cannot always be placed on maps, while air reconnaissance, except over the more open routes and areas, is unlikely to locate hostile troops. The passage of information from patrols is slow and sometimes, due to delay, loses much of its value. Information may be obtained from local inhabitants, especially if cash for buying it is available in the hands of forward commanders, but it is not always reliable and must be treated with caution.

8. First contact may be gained by special reconnoitring patrols, sent to obtain information on which to base manoeuvre, or by long range detachments sent to ambush the enemy and delay his advance.

9. When contact by advancing columns appear imminent, security measures must be increased with strong fighting patrols to the flanks. When contact is gained, a special effort must be made immediately to determine the enemy strength and dispositions, particularly the location of his flanks. At this stage, as, in fact, in all operations in jungle, commanders must be well forward to receive early information and to initiate prompt aggressive action. In this way surprise may be effected through the enemy having insufficient

time to determine the direction and strength of the movements being made against him. This too is the stage at which good battle drill will achieve big results by tactical moves being carried out rapidly and automatically by junior leaders who know what is expected of them and take action on their own initiative. This type of battle drill is described in the "Instructor's Handbook on Fieldcraft and Battle Drill (India)" and "Battle Drills for Dense Jungle".

VII. THE ATTACK.

1. **The Encounter Battle.**—Offensive tactics in the jungle always pay because the attacker can approach the enemy position closely before being detected, and can thereby gain initially the advantage of surprise. Once surprise has been effected, the tactical plan must be developed quickly with the realization that the longer the period of its preparation the more time will the enemy have in which to gain information of the attack and to make his dispositions to counter it. During the period of preparation for the attack troops not in contact with the enemy must be so disposed that they can resist and immediately counter-attack any endeavour by the enemy to outflank or envelop them.

In the encounter battle, artillery and mortar fire may have its best effect by being directed on the enemy axis of advance to disorganize him and delay his movement. Air attack on the enemy axis will also assist at this time.

The difficult problem in using artillery and mortars is observation of fire; this is considered in Chapter V. Ranging and observation may be possible from trees or from air O.Ps., or, in the case of a coastal area, from the water. F.O.Os. Must accompany patrols in order to direct long range fire on to approaching enemy columns.

In general, attacks must be made on a narrow front in order to maintain control. Gaps between units must be covered by patrols to prevent enemy moves being made unseen.

A firm base from which the battle is conducted must be established on, or near, the axis of advance, with a strong reserve in hand to meet eventualities.

Once the troops are committed to the attack on any particular objective, they must continue until it is captured. To halt and try to take cover is fatal; it results in high casualties and failure to take the objective.

2. **Frontal and Flanking Attacks.**—In general, there are two forms of attack: the front and the flanking attack—

(a) The frontal attack may be employed when time or the nature of the country does not permit outflanking, or when the enemy is over-extended. The attack may often be made astride the axis of advance as this simplifies control and direction, and enables supporting weapons to be employed quickly. To avoid exposing themselves, troops must keep clear of the actual track and move under cover along both sides.

(b) The outflanking attack is more difficult than the front attack but it may often be decisive.

The outflanking attack will normally be carried out by dividing a force into four main components. The first component consists of the fixing element, which secures the track, or some tactical feature, and fixes the enemy. The second and third components are the outflanking elements which make the main attack on one or both of the enemy's flanks or on his rear. The fourth component is the reserve, the size of which must be sufficient to exploit the success of either or both of the other two forces, and counter any hostile reactions.

In order to help outflanking attacks, vigorous action by the fixing force is necessary. This may deceive the enemy as to the point of the main attack, and cause him to employ his reserve prematurely.

It will frequently be necessary for the commander to detail a special force for the flank protection of the outflanking component.

Units making the outflanking attack must adopt a formation that will provide all-round protection. All-round protection is provided by patrols, scouts and observers. When observation is limited and there are few landmarks, maintenance of direction is difficult. For this reason, changes of direction should be made by compass bearing and curved approach should not be attempted.

To maintain control, and to check direction, short bounds are necessary. Checkers of direction and distance should be specially detailed. Bounds may be fixed by time, by distance, or by movements from one feature to another that can be seen and pointed out on the ground.

Unless wireless communication is reliable, and even then as an additional precaution, companies and larger units should lay signal cable as they advance.

On contact being gained, or on arrival in a prearranged area, deployment will automatically be carried out according to the battle drill of the commander.

The attack may result in a series of engagements by small parties at close range. Troops must react promptly and energetically, remembering that the attack must always be made with speed and determination.

Once the attack is under way, the commander can exert but little influence except by the effective employment of the reserve. The probable area in which the reserve will be used must be anticipated so that it can be employed without loss of time. Whenever possible the reserve should be employed as a complete unit.

3. **Attacks against minor resistance.**—When only minor resistance is encountered, the advanced guard must dispose of the enemy quickly by the rapid and determined execution of one of the prearranged battle drills. Leading sub-units must obtain cover by leaving the track at once, and must then move towards the enemy on their own allotted routes and with their own protective elements. Action must include direct action by fire and, when practicable, flanking action against one or both flanks. At this stage great reliance is placed on junior leaders, who must accomplish their task in their own sectors without waiting for the assistance of adjacent sub-units.

Sometimes it may be desirable to "by pass" minor resistance. In this case the original advanced guard will usually fix and isolate the enemy while the main body continues the advance with a new advanced guard by making a detour round the enemy.

4. **Attacks against prepared positions.**—In the attack against prepared positions, it is necessary to develop a plan which includes the fullest possible use of all supporting arms and weapons.

Thorough reconnaissance to determine the location of the enemy strong points, including the exact position of automatic weapons, is of the utmost importance. On many occasions it may be necessary to fight for this information, if necessary by staging a preliminary attack. Patrols and observers by day, and patrols right into the enemy's lines by night, can obtain this information if they are well led and use cunning and stratagem to draw the enemy's fire. Special features which patrols and observers should examine for Japanese positions are: all high ground from which observation and a good field of fire can be obtained; trees, particularly at road or track bends; culverts; the edge of clearings; the openings underneath native huts, and the roofs of buildings. Areas on the flanks of restricted approaches, such as dry stream beds or a single route through swamps or heavy jungle, should be carefully examined.

Based on the information of patrols the commander will develop his fire plan to bring the maximum possible concentration to bear on a comparatively narrow front. A thick barrage on a narrow front may frequently prove to be the best form of artillery support.

DECEPTION IN THE ATTACK.

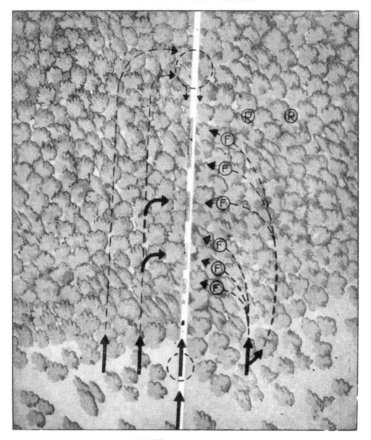

LEGEND.

(R)   Reconnaissance Patrol (3 men)

(F)   Fighting Patrol (9 or more men)

Strong and fast fighting patrol action on flank to deceive the enemy while the main attack develops on the opposite flank and rear.

A limited objective should be assigned in order to ensure proper consolidation and adequate mopping up.

The value of air support will often depend on the extent to which troops and pilots have worked together in jungle areas, especially in the area in which operations are taking place. The indication of targets to pilots by use of smoke, flares or other signals, and the reporting of targets by pilots, presents special difficulties that can be overcome effectively only by previous combined training amounting to close personal friendship.

When tanks are available and ground is suitable for their use they will be of both moral and material value in the close support of infantry, especially if their employment can come as a surprise. The heavy gun of the larger types of tanks should be particularly effective against Japanese emplacements of the "bunker" type. The opportunities which the jungle affords for the action of tank hunting parties demand, however, that infantry and tanks work in even closer co-operation than in more open country and it will rarely be advisable to despatch an echelon of tanks alone to the objective.

5. **Phases of an attack against a prepared position.**—Large scale attacks of the nature described above may be divided into two preparatory and three battle phases.

Phase "A".—*Preparatory.*—This may extend over several days. Its object is to obtain the detailed lay-out of the Jap defences and their fire plan. This is accomplished by aggressive patrolling and counter-sniping combined with organized observation, ruses and dummy attacks by day and night to draw fire. The R.A.F. will play an important part in this observation and should get to know the area well. It may be possible to indicate targets by the use of coloured smoke.

Units that will be employed in the attack must take every opportunity of studying the ground over which they will attack, and should rehearse details of the attack on similar ground in an area in rear. Infantry, artillery, engineers, tanks and R.A.F. must all practice together.

Phase "B".—*Preparatory.*—This may take place during the night preceding the attack and may consist of:

(i) Protection of forming up positions, start lines, etc. This will include gaining control of the approaches to the Japanese positions.

(ii) Steps to ensure the accurate maintenance of direction.

(iii) Movement of supporting weapons into position, and their concealment.

(iv) Provision of flank protection.

(v) Preliminary arrangements for gapping wire and minefields.

(vi) Deceptive measures, including the continuance of normal activity.

(vii) Under certain circumstances infiltration of specially selected personnel into and through the enemy position.

Phase "C".—The Battle.—This phase may comprise:—

(i) Direct air support, and constant air reconnaissance over enemy reserve and rear areas.

(ii) Barrage by artillery and other supporting weapons. Lifts of 100 yards every 3 minutes have been suitable in average jungle. Dense jungle will demand a slower rate of lift.

(iii) Smoke for deception or to cover the advance in certain areas.

(iv) *The Assault.*—The actual assault may have the following sequence :—

(*a*) Infantry pioneers or engineers clear gaps through wire defences.

(*b*) Special assault parties of infantry and pioneers or engineers blind enemy pill boxes or "bunkers" by sandbags or explosives placed in loop holes. Spare parties are necessary to deal with previously unlocated "bunkers".

(*c*) First wave of infantry passes through to objective killing as it goes but not halting to mop up. It consolidates immediately, pushes out patrols and prepares to meet the inevitable counter-attack.

(*d*) Other pioneer or engineer parties and moppers up following closely on (*c*) above. Pioneers and engineers destroy pill boxes and "bunkers" with explosives. Moppers up complete the destruction of defenders with bullet, bayonet and bomb.

Seeing that the Japanese are likely to bring down defensive fire on their own positions it is essential that every man and every party should have a specific task and be drilled in it, so that mopping up can be done speedily and thoroughly and so that personnel do not have to remain too long on the enemy position during the enemy defensive fire.

Phase "D".—Consolidation.—The Japanese will probably counter attack a position within a few minutes of its capture. To be ready for such counter attacks, defensive fire must be pre-arranged if possible, and the plan for consolidation decided in advance. This plan must include arrangements for sending out fighting patrols bringing up tools and supporting weapons, and for organising all round defence in depth.

Phase "E".—Exploitation.—The plan for exploitation is dependent on several factors. Some of these are: the extent to which the enemy has been broken, or demoralised, by the attack; the depth of the enemy position;

the necessity for seizing quickly any tactical feature beyond the immediate objective; the artillery support required to cover consolidation; the time available, bearing in mind that an attacking force must have sufficient time in which to form a defended area for the night. The aim, however, must always be establish a firm base first, and then, when that has been done, to deliver the subsequent thrust as rapidly as possible.

VIII. THE DEFENCE.

1. **General.**—Although, when training troops for jungle warfare, it is necessary to devote great attention to offensive tactics, training in defence must not be neglected. A temporary assumption of the defensive may on occasions be necessary, while it is always necessary in the form of protection at rest at the completion of a day's advance, and at the end of each day's fighting. A passive defence must, however, never be permitted. The very essence of defence in dense country is that it must be both mobile and aggressive. Defended localities are required, but their chief purpose is to provide firm bases from which mobile elements operate for laying ambushes, for offensive patrolling and for immediate counter attack. Strong reserves, prepared for offensive action, must be located where they can move immediately to any threatened locality.

2. **Occupation of a position for the night**.—A minimum of two hours of daylight must be allowed for the establishment of a position for the night so that preparations may be completed before darkness.

The "harbour" will be organised as a perimeter defence. As a guide, the force will normally be divided into the following parts:—

(a) One-half for perimeter defence, of which a third will be disposed in depth to counter infiltration.

(b) One quarter in reserve for immediate counter attack to expel any penetration.

(c) One quarter for counter offensive action against such enemy as are located by patrols, snipers or listening posts outside the perimeter. This part may frequently form its own "harbour" outside, but within supporting distance of the perimeter. In these circumstances its methods will be similar to that of a detached force.

Slit trenches will be dug for each rifle and Bren Group to give protection against enemy bombing, artillery and mortar fire; in addition they permit the

ACTIVE DEFENCE.

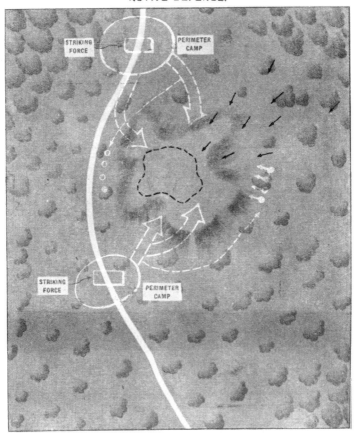

The object is to destroy the enemy.

defender to make the maximum use of hand grenades which are very effective night weapons.

Fields of fire will be developed by cutting lanes for the fire of all weapons, Such lanes should be cut with the object of increasing fields of view and fire, and when time permits, some form of obstruction such as "panjis" should be erected on the rear side of the lane to hold under fire any enemy crossing the fire lane. When the denseness of the jungle is suitable, fire lanes will be cut only knee high in the form of tunnels. In this way the approaching Japanese will be unaware that he is entering a fire lane, unless he is crawling, and the defensive posts will not be disclosed.

Trip wires (creepers), booby traps and warning devices should be erected to prevent the enemy from infiltrating unheard. Enemy who approach the position by night will be disposed of with the bayonet or grenade.

Unless the enemy attempts to rush a position, firing at night should be forbidden. Usually the objects of enemy fire at night are to discover the position of sentries and posts, to disturb the defenders and to inflict loss. If fire is not returned he will fail in his first two objects; and he is unlikely to be successful in the third.

At dusk and at first light all men will "stand to".

3. **Active Defence.**—The enemy will usually seek to employ outflanking tactics. It must be remembered that these tactics generally entail the disadvantages of a long advance, with long routes of supply, difficulties of communications, and movement in country which is not known to the attackers. The defenders, on the other hand, are fighting on ground of their own choosing, they will usually have shorter and better communications, with better control and with reserves centralised. With these advantages, a mobile, aggressive, well handled defence will have opportunities to destroy the enemy in the jungle, and this is the task of the counter offensive part of the garrison. Meanwhile, the garrison of the firm bases from which the counter offensive troops are operating will hold out to the last man, and every man in every locality must know that, by so doing, he is assisting in the plan to destroy the enemy while others are co-operating with him. Every man whatever his army and employment, must be trained to fight.

The main problem of the defence in jungle is to prevent infiltration. To overcome this, patrols and snipers must operate forward of localities. The role of these patrols is not only to provide information as to the action of the enemy, his strength and direction of approach, but also to harass and hit him should he approach. Patrols may also be given the role of denying the enemy reconnaissance of the position. No enemy reconnaissance if in any way careless will survive in the face of highly organised and well concealed snipers.

The use of ambushes for surprising the enemy and disorganising his attacks is dealt with in Chapter IX.

In the case of mobile, detached forces, trails will be avoided and a suitable position may often be found in an extra thick patch of jungle. Protection will then be provided by a system of all-round localities with piquets on the likely approaches and vantage points, and local patrols. Unless the force is very small, it must not be camped in one locality, since this gives the enemy an opportunity to surround it, and to concentrate his fire on the necessarily crowded space inside. The lay-out of localities in the form of a starfish has the advantage that the reserve is placed centrally, and communications run outwards from the centre. This arrangement also makes infiltration both difficult and dangerous for the enemy.

4. **Position Defence.**—There are occasions in the jungle when a more permanent type of defence has to be undertaken. Under these circumstances, the position selected should be on ground of vital tactical importance which cannot be "by-passed" with impunity.

Since artillery support will generally be limited, the position should provide for the maximum use of all infantry weapons, particularly the flanking fire of automatics. The defence should then be built around the automatic weapons, using the minimum number of men necessary to operate and protect them. The posts must be mutually supporting and sited in tactical localities both laterally and in depth. Localities must be self contained and with sufficient water, rations and ammunition to enable them to last for several days without assistance. Advantage should be taken of natural obstacles and of the opportunities the jungle affords for the erection of artificial obstacles. Communications must be arranged both laterally and in depth to provide for the rapid movement of reserves. The additional time available for the preparation of the position will allow considerable clearing of fields of fire and this must come high in priority of work to be done.

Complete concealment of the position is essential to prevent the enemy from locating posts and weapons; the most effective means of screening is by natural camouflage from the neighbouring jungle. Both ground and tree snipers must be employed to prevent reconnaissance by enemy patrols and fire from concealed posts must be withheld until an assault is made in force and the enemy arrives at point blank killing range.

The conduct of the defence must be aggressive. This is achieved by allotting as large a proportion of the force as possible for counter attack. When the time arrives for launching the counter attack, it must go in with the minimum delay possible. In order to be able to do so previous reconnaissance and rehearsal are essential. In dense jungle it may be also necessary to cut tracks beforehand and in any case routes should be marked.

The cover afforded by jungle will facilitate the concealed approach of the counter attack and enable it more easily to achieve surprise.

The speed with which a counter attack can be launched will depend on the size of the force engaged and the completeness of the previous preparations.

IX. AMBUSHES.

1. Due to his rapid method of advance along jungle tracks, often with inadequate protection, the Jap is especially susceptible to ambushes.

2. An ambush is like any other operation of war. A leader preparing an ambush must appreciate the situation by asking himself what is his object, by considering the factors and making a plan. No one ambush will ever be like any other. The second principle to remember is that an ambush relies for its success entirely upon surprise.

3. Thirdly, an ambush must have a reserve to take advantage of favourable opportunities and deal with the unexpected.

4. Let us consider in the light of recent experience the average Japanese reaction to ambush. It has been stereotyped and is therefore predictable:—

(*a*) His leading elements get off the path and try an outflanking movement.

(*b*) He brings his mortar into action (and he is seldom unaccompanied by a mortar) with the least possible delay and attacks astride the track the area in which the ambush has been laid. This sometimes takes place in as short a time as five minutes.

It follows that in most cases, unless arrangements are made to the contrary, the Jap is left in possession of the battlefield and is thus able to dispose of our wounded, to collect his own, and to stop us getting identification. This has happened frequently in the past. Any plan of laying an ambush therefore should always bear in mind the desirability or otherwise of remaining in possession of the battlefield. This is particularly the case where identifications are required.

. 5. On an ambush taking place and a fight ensuing there will inevitably be some confusion and an R.V. is therefore necessary for the ambushing party.

TYPES OF AMBUSHES

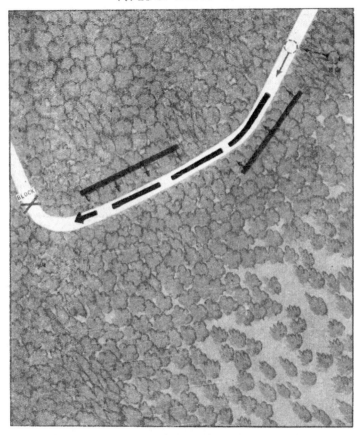

QUICK AMBUSH

It may take some hours before all the ambushing party collects at the R.V. It is all the more clear therefore that if we are to take advantage of the situation particularly during the period of confusion the reserve should be brought into action and boldly handled.

6. The relative strengths of the ambushing party and the reserve is a matter for consideration and this is really affected by the object. If the object is merely

to cause confusion and then carry out the main fighting by the reserve then the actual ambushing party can be very small indeed, possibly one leader and two men. If on the other hand it is known that the enemy about to be ambushed are in large numbers, more in fact than could be dealt with by a very small ambushing party, it is clear that the ambush party itself will have to be in sufficient strength to deal with them, and in fact will be sub-divided into two or three or more sub-units. An example of what has been carried out in the Chin Hills for instance is for the reserve, after the ambush has been carried out, to go ahead in the direction from which the Japs have advanced and destroy the Japanese mortar which always comes into action, generally about 1,000 yards back.

7. The following factors based on experience should be borne in mind:—

(*a*) When ambushed Jap soldiers have been known to drop and lie doggo feigning dead, where they will lie still for long periods. Like dealing with any other dangerous game it will be found advisable to ensure that they ARE dead either by bullet or bayonet or both.

(*b*) The use of "panjis" has been found to be most effective. They are placed parallel to the track and just off it inside the jungle so that the Japs who scatter on being ambushed find themselves impaled. This has been proved to be very successful.

(*c*) *Baits.*—In one ambush an old Japanese steel helmet was left on the track as a bait. The Japanese stopped and collected round this helmet asking questions and examining it, thus giving our men the opportunity they needed of increasing the "bag" and providing a concentrated target at short range almost justifying the employment of automatic fire.

(*d*) The ambush party may be on one side of the track or on both sides. In the former case the enemy may disappear on the far side and here "Panjis" would be found effective. In the latter case there is always the danger of the ambush parties firing on each other. A practical solution has been found by having the ambush parties on both sides of the track "staggered". The ground will generally dictate the answer to this problem.

(*e*) Where the ambush is laid on a hill-side there may be a question as to whether it should be laid up-hill or down-hill of the enemy, or a bit of both. Up-hill puts the ambushing party in the more advantageous position, but on the other hand the enemy will disappear more quickly down-hill than up. A few snipers suitably disposed can take care of this, particularly if the ambush is laid in a re-entrant.

TYPES OF AMBUSHES.

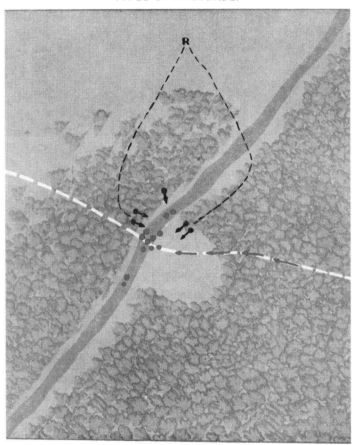

AMBUSH AT A WATER HOLE

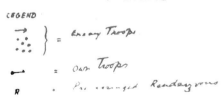

LEGEND

→ } = Enemy Troops
∴∵

•— = Own Troops

R = Pre-arranged Rendezvous

45

TYPES OF AMBUSHES.

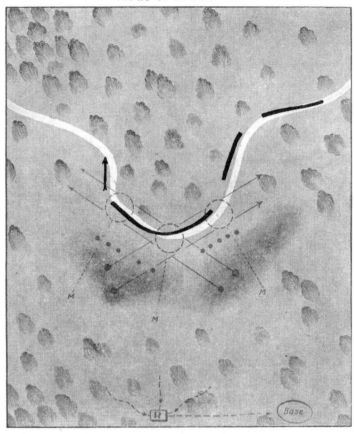

AMBUSH AT A BEND IN THE TRACK

LEGEND :

   M   = Mortar
   ◌   = Concentration of Mortar fire
   R   = Pre arranged Rendezvous
   →   = L.M.G. Fire

Note: The reserve has not been shown.

(*f*) *Foot-marks.*—These have constantly to be borne in mind. Foot-marks give the show away more than anything else. The problem of laying an ambush on a dusty track without giving away the fact that we have been there needs very careful consideration indeed. It will often be found advisable to approach the ambush position by cutting one's way through the jungle for some distance back. Another alternative is to approach barefooted. Many other methods can be thought out but the question of foot-marks is one which must be given prior consideration. Neglect to consider this question may result in the ambush being a costly failure.

(*g*) The order to open fire must clearly be given only by the commander of the ambush party. His position will depend largely on circumstances but he should usually be in such a place that he can personally count the number of rats he has got in the trap.

X. PATROLLING

"The side which wins the patrolling encounter wins the battle."
(Quotation from Report on Milne Bay Operation.)

1. **General.**—Patrolling is a very wide term. In jungle warfare, where the lack of communications forces the use of smaller bodies of troops, patrolling has a wider application than ever. It is in effect the technique of moving and fighting over long distances and for periods which may extend to ten days or even more, of bodies of troops up to one company.

Patrol tactics are in some respects similar to air tactics. Just as in the air it is necessary to create a favourable air situation for other air operations by concentrating superior fighting forces, in order to clear the enemy out of the air and thereby to permit further uninterrupted air operations or reconnaissance, so on the ground before uninterrupted reconnaissance can be carried out, it is essential that the country between you and the enemy however extensive this may be, should be made "Your man's land" rather than "No man's land". To do this, it is essential that on every occasion you must produce superior forces against the enemy, so that you can destroy the enemy, dominate the battlefield, however small this may be, and remain masers of it. Therefore, if experience shows that the Jap patrols are normally 5 or 6, then yours should be 15 or 20; if the Jap sends 30 or 40, send a company. Only in this way are you certain so to dominate the country that your reconnaissance patrols can move

DESTROYING ENEMY SNIPERS BY DAY.

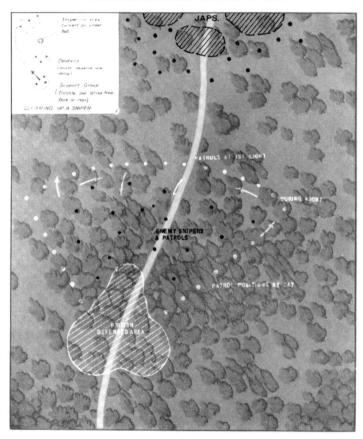

Snipers may be encouraged to encroach into the area by lack of patrolling for a few nights. The area can then be cleared by intensive anti-sniper patrols working as shown.

unmolested, infiltrate where they will and provide you with just that detailed information, which the first class plan demands.

These fighting patrols have the object of gaining "ground superiority" and this they will achieve most quickly by always being the first to surprise the Japs. Unless he is a jungle fighter of the highest standard, the moving man is generally at the mercy of the man who lies in wait. Our patrols should therefore, be stationary when contact is made or as soon after as possible. To carry out their task, however, movement is normally essential.

This difficulty can be overcome by two methods:—

(a) formation

(b) battle drill

Correct formation will provide adequate warning of the approach of the enemy and, if the leading troops are skilled in observation on the move, of the enemy concealed in ambush. Correct battle drill will ensure that the most rapid deployment into ambush positions is made as a result of the information provided in (a).

Should the Japanese in any sector prove supine on patrol, it may be necessary to lay a bait, such as the burning of a hut of an enemy agent in order to whet his curiosity and to encourage him to move out to investigate. Other methods will suggest themselves. Patrols should not be stereotyped in the ambushes they lay. When a small enemy party is expected and our patrol has superiority in numbers it may be best to put a large proportion of the force into "the shop window" of the ambush, with the object of killing all the enemy in reserve. At other times it may be preferable to use only two or three men to "spring the trap", whilst the remainder, held in reserve, sidestep the inevitable Jap counter attack and destroy it from the flank or rear.

The permutations and combinations of the "two fisted" methods of fighting patrols are as inexhaustible in the jungle as they are in the ring.

After every patrol clash in the jungle it is essential that our patrol should remain in complete, if only temporary, possession of the battlefield. This is necessary in order that our patrol may collect identifications and remove enemy wounded, who always talk. This can only be achieved by hard fighting and the complete defeat of the whole of the opposing patrol.

2. **R.V.'s.**—It is clear that patrol clashes of this sort in jungle must inevitable lead to some loss of control and men may find themselves separated from their comrades and not knowing where the remainder of the patrol is. For this reason every patrol must have a R.V. to which, if control is lost, personnel will make their own way.

The technique of the selection of R.V.'s is an important part of patrol leadership and must be studied by all junior commanders. Examples are given below:—

(a) When advancing to carry out a patrol task R.V.s will normally always be selected in a place which can be easily recognised by the troops. With highly trained troops it may well be possible to select a R.V. in a forward direction so that patrols can continue once control is regained without any loss of time or distance. When, however, the troops are less highly trained it may even be necessary to select the last halting place as the R.V.

AN ENCOUNTER WITH THE ENEMY EN ROUTE MUST NEVER DETER A PATROL FROM COMPLETING ITS TASK.

(b) When returning from a patrol task, R.V.'s will normally be towards our own lines.

As individual infiltration to a R.V. within our own lines makes the task of defensive sentries particularly difficult, control should normally be re-established before reaching our lines by the selection of a R.V. outside the range of the listening posts or protective patrols of the firm base.

(c) When the commander is aware that his patrol is being trailed by the enemy, it may be advisable to select a R.V. in an unexpected direction and thereafter by a detour to resume the original direction of the patrol.

(d) It cannot be too strongly emphasized that every patrol whether of 2 hours or 10 days' duration must be planned in detail as a series of bounds. Each bound must have its own R.V. and every member of the patrol must be clear what that R.V. is.

(e) Patrol Commanders must realise that they may have maps and compasses, whereas their men probably have neither. Selected R.V.'s must therefore, be unmistakable on the ground. Each man should have a rough sketch of the main features of the area in which he is working so that he knows where to go if he is completely lost. For instance a main river, the principal hills and subsidiary streams would be sufficient with the distances marked from one point to another. Such a sketch would not take more than five minutes to make.

It is often advisable to R.V. not in an area but at a point on a line and there seems to be much to commend this. It is necessary however that people should stay at R.V.'s sufficiently long to collect stragglers, otherwise the men will cease to have confidence in them. Here again a line appears to be a suitable type of R.V. as men can move along a line from point to point so as not to stay too long in one place and risk being caught.

R.V.'s themselves must be constantly patrolled, and in fact should be one moveable ambush.

3. **Resting.**—Never rest nearer than is necessary to a village or a track. If, however, the force is sufficiently strong it may be desirable to have a small post on the nearest track which will be able to give information to passers-by and warning of the enemy. This post according to the situation could be either for watching purposes only, or combine that with an ambush.

Never rest too long in one place but keep moving on. When fires have been lit to cook tea, etc., it is best afterwards to move a mile or so before dossing down for the night.

Always clean up a camp site before moving. Cigarette packets, etc., not only give away the fact that one has been there recently but are apt also to be an indication of your numbers. To leave litter is to leave a letter to an intelligent enemy as to your strength and intention.

4. **Tracks.**—Experience has shown that either all movement should be done off the tracks or a risk should be taken and moves done so boldly and fast along the tracks, that the patrol travels faster than the news of its movements. Circumstances may dictate the necessity for using tracks but patrols must recognise that by so doing they are constantly in danger of ambushes.

Foot-marks and boot-marks give the show away. The Japs wear rubber-soled boots with zig-zag markers which are easily recognized. It is also easy to recognize the difference between our hob-nailed boots and those of the enemy. The experienced tracker can tell whether marks are fresh or not. Consequently, when using the paths, one runs the danger not only of being ambushed but of being followed up and hunted. There are three methods which have been used to avoid this latter alternative—

(a) To go barefoot.

(b) To leave the track altogether, but even this gives indications as to the point at which one has left the track and even in the jungle itself footmarks are visible.

(c) A successful alternative has been to leave the track by walking *backwards* off the track into the jungle and sending some people on to walk *forwards* off the track into the jungle on the opposite side. The result of this would be that if one wants to leave the path to the left one should show marks of having left it to the right and going in the opposite direction. There must be many other opportunities for cunning of this kind.

5. **Reaction to surprise.**—However well trained a patrol may be, it may one day find itself surprised, seeing that jungle makes surprise easy. The quicker

the reaction, both individual and collective, to that surprise the less will be its effect. It is imperative, therefore, that every patrol should have an immediate action battledrill if ambushed, as the result of which every man individually and the patrol as a whole will take some immediate offensive action, normally with the bayonet, which not only will extract the patrol from the ambush but also will destroy a part, if not all, of the ambushing party.

By night, dispersal is fatal. Troops must be made to realise that fire by night is unaimed, and that the best thing they can do is to sit tight exactly where they are so that the commander may be able to control them and give such orders as are necessary.

6. **Strength of Patrols.**—The strength of a patrol depends on its tasks. If it is a reconnoitring patrol it should be just as big as is required and no more. It is seldom likely to be less than one leader and two men. If, however, the patrol is likely to meet the enemy when on the move and is likely to have to defend itself it should obviously be in sufficient strength to do so. Japanese patrols are normally 30–50 men strong, with a mortar detachment, i.e., a strong Platoon. It follows that either our patrols must be as strong or stronger, or else they should be so small that they can "fade" and evade the action while keeping the enemy under observation.

The strength of a patrol is also affected by the distance which it has to operate—for instance it may be out for as long as ten days or more, i.e., four days out, four days back and two days operating. If this is the case it has to carry a considerable amount of weight in rations, ammunition, mosquito nets, waterproof sheets, etc. This being the case the patrol should form at a convenient point a small defended advanced base from which "firm base" the final patrolling will be carried out. In this case in addition to the number of men required to do the actual final patrolling sufficient will have to be added to carry the extra rations, etc., to the "firm base" and to protect it. It will also probably be necessary to include a wireless set and a medical orderly. All this means meticulous administrative planning. The main principle however remains—that a reconnoitring patrol should normally be so small as to be capable of "fading" if the enemy is contacted, and keeping him under observation, or of being in sufficient strength to defeat the enemy patrol if encountered.

7. **Intelligence Personnel and Local Inhabitants.**—Patrols of the nature described above will normally be accompanied by a detachment of the Burma Intelligence Corps whose duty it will be to gain local information by talking to the inhabitants or by enlisting the help of local guides.

8. **Animals.**—It may be necessary to use mules or pack ponies to accompany the patrol as far as the firm base but it must be remembered that

their maintenance and protection is generally an added complication. In some cases elephants have been usefully employed with patrols for carrying such things as a wireless set and the heavier items of baggage such as waterproof sheets, but here again there are difficulties as elephants cannot march all day and they must have time off in which to collect their own food.

9. **Tasks of Long Distance Patrols.**—Long distance patrols such as outlined above have a wide variety of tasks. It is in fact difficult to classify every variety, and each patrol must be organised strictly in accordance with its task. Examples, however, are as under:—

(a) *Routine Area Patrols*—These are commonly used to see if the enemy is or is not operating in a certain area. They are generally small in numbers. They obtain their information partly by the use of local guides and questioning of inhabitants, and partly by general observation. Although they are "routine" patrols they should never follow the same route twice nor should they go on certain days of the week or at certain hours of the day.

(b) *Connecting Patrols.*—These may be used between defended areas in the same way as used to be done in previous outpost positions. They should normally be strong enough to tackle any enemy encountered.

(c) *Long Distance Patrols.*—These are normally sent out for a specific task, e.g., to report on the dispositions of the enemy known to be in a certain area, or to kidnap a Jap or a local inhabitant for purposes of interrogation from an area in which the enemy is known to be living. Such patrols will normally operate from a firm base of their own making.

(d) *Prolonged Observation Patrols.*—These may be employed to watch a stretch of river, each observation patrol being given its mileage of front linking up with those on its right and left. Such patrols should be as small in numbers as possible, the main consideration here being good communications back to the firm base from which they are operating.

The above list is by no means exhaustive. The tasks on which long distance patrols of this nature may be sent are legion.

10. **Planning.**—A patrol commander on being given orders for his patrol must appreciate the situation and make a plan the same as for any other operation of war. He must have his object clearly fixed in his mind, and if his object is not clear he must ask his superior officer to clarify it so that there can be no doubt whatever. He must be told what to do if he meets the enemy. He must realise that administrative problems will form a most important part of his planning. It is essential that the longer the distance and the greater the hardships likely to be encountered the more careful the administrative

arrangements should be. He must remember that it is his duty to bring his patrol fresh to the sphere of operations. It may suit him if desirable to include in his programme a complete rest for 24 hours at his firm base before he starts operations.

11. **Action on Meeting the Enemy.**—This must be clearly defined in the mind of every man in the patrol. Either the enemy must be fought and killed or he must be watched and dogged and his every movement reported. A patrol which on meeting the enemy breaks contact and returns, and reports that it has met the enemy and broken contact of its own volition has neglected its duty and is subject to disciplinary action.

12. **Clothing.**—Reduce clothing and equipment of patrols to an irreducible minimum and then reduce them again. Rope or rubber-soled shoes or boots should be worn unless the patrol is a very long-distance one, in which case it will be better to wear boots up to the point from which the actual patrolling takes place. Uniform should be dyed green in patches, alternating with khaki.

13. **Miscellaneous.**—Never send a man out from a patrol on his own more than a few yards. It is extraordinary how men get lost. Sometimes even after fifty yards men get lost and are not seen again, possibly for some days, possibly never.

Regard the local inhabitants with suspicion. They are always prepared to pass on information about you. If you meet the odd local in some out-of-the-way place take him along with you for a couple of days and turn him loose when he can do you no harm. You may find in the meantime he will be quite useful in many small ways.

Remember that Jap patrols are very often preceded by local inhabitants, acting as scouts, and take whatever action seems necessary in the circumstances.

XI. WITHDRAWAL.
THERE WILL BE NO WITHDRAWAL.

Field Manual 72-20
Jungle Warfare

Section I. TRAINING FOR JUNGLE SERVICE

Physical Conditioning

a. During training for jungle operations, continuous emphasis must be placed on physical conditioning. Officers and men must follow a strict program designed to increase stamina. In the final periods of training all work should be in the field. Difficult tactical marches constitute good conditioning exercises. Tactical exercises should be conducted over the most difficult terrain available. Swimming is one of the best all-around exercises; jungle training areas frequently include swimming facilities. Obstacle courses of the ordinary type provide another excellent means of conditioning.

b. ACCLIMATIZATION. (1) Prior to entering a jungle combat area, troops from temperate zones should undergo a special period of training, gradually increasing in hardship, in a jungle area of similar climate and terrain to that in which they are to fight. This training period is required regardless of the physical condition of the troops, although good physical condition will permit considerable shortening of the period. For seasoned troops, a period of four weeks should suffice. Longer periods result in staleness and a decrease in efficiency. The general health, and hence the effectiveness of a command subject to strenuous exertion and poor living conditions in the tropics, degenerates progressively with the passage of time. Ideally, therefore, the period of training should be conducted in a tropical or subtropical area thoroughly controlled by friendly troops; movement to the combat zone should be planned to permit arrival of the troops only early enough before being committed to action to allow a brief tune-up following the period of inactivity during travel; one week should be sufficient time for this tune-up.

(2) When work is begun at the time of first exposure to the heat and progressively increased with the limits of tolerance of the man, full acclimatization (the ability to perform a maximum amount of strenuous work in the heat) is attained most quickly. A schedule, with alternating rest and work periods of one-half hour, and which provides for work during the cooler morning hours and in the hot afternoon hours, should be set up according to the following plan:

Proposed Schedule of Work During Period of Acclimatization

When maximum air temp. is 90° to 105° F.	Hours of work	When maximum air temp. is 105° F. and over
First day	0700–0900 and 1500–1700	0700–0900 and 1500–1600
Second day	0700–1000 and 1430–1630	0700–1000 and 1500–1600
Third day	0700–1000 and 1400–1700	0700–1000 and 1400–1600
Fourth day	0700–1100 and 1330–1750	0700–1000 and 1330–1630
Fifth day	Regular duty	0700–1100 and 1330–1630
Sixth day	Regular duty	Regular duty

(3) Once acclimatized, the soldier will retain his adaptation for from one to two weeks after he leaves the hot environment. If not reexposed to high temperatures, the acclimatization will then decrease at a variable rate. Most men lose the major portion of their acclimatization in one month.

(4) The well-acclimatized man deprived of adequate rest at night is incapable of producing his customary amount of work in the heat on the ensuing day, or does so less efficiently.

(5) Officers who know the work capacities of their men can determine their degree of acclimatization and whether or not it is safe for them to continue activity. The acclimatized man is alert, performs his work energetically and without symptoms. In contrast, the unacclimatized man working in the heat becomes dull and apathetic, performs his work poorly, and may manifest to varying degrees, either singly or in combination, the symptoms and signs of heat exhaustion.

c. WATER REQUIREMENTS. (1) In the jungle, where the humidity is high, sweat does not evaporate but runs off the skin; therefore, cooling is less efficient and water losses may be greater.

(2) At high temperatures a resting man may lose as much as a pint of water per hour during the day by sweating; if he works, his water loss (and requirement) will increase in direct proportion to the amount of work done. Hardworking personnel, such as engineers, marching men, and members of labor battalions, may require as much as 3 gallons of water per man per day. Any restriction of water below the levels necessary for the men will result in rapid loss of efficiency, reduction in ability to work, and deterioration in morale. If restriction is continued for hours, temperatures will rise and heat exhaustion occur. There is no advantage in using thirst quenchers

such as chewing gum, fruit drops, etc. For a given amount of work under high temperature conditions, it has been found that water consumption is substantially the same whether water is taken only at meal times or taken when thirsty. The greatest benefit will be obtained and maximum efficiency result if water is taken at short rather than at long intervals. Drinking in small amounts when thirsty is the ideal practice.

d. SALT REQUIREMENTS. In all circumstances, the loss of a large volume of water through sweat is associated with a loss of salt. The amounts of salt taken in the normal diet are adequate to supply and make up for the losses when the total water intake is under 1 gallon per day. Above these levels, added salt is needed. It is best taken in solution in the drinking water. It is particularly necessary that salt be taken in the first few days of exposure to heat, since the losses of salt then are greater than after acclimatization. Water containing the proper amount of salt can be prepared as follows:

(1) One pound table salt to 100 gallons of water.

(2) 0.3 of a pound table salt to the Lyster bag (36 gallons).

(3) One-fourth teaspoonful table salt to each canteen of water.

(4) Two 10-grain salt tablets dissolved in every quart of water consumed. The consumption of undissolved salt tablets is not recommended.

e. HEAT STROKE, HEAT EXHAUSTION AND HEAT CRAMPS. (1) *General.* Troops training or operating in hot climates may experience one or more of the ill effects of exposure to high temperatures. This is more likely to occur if there is also a high humidity. There are three well-defined conditions which should be understood by all line officers and enlisted men. These are: (a) heat stroke, (b) heat exhaustion, (c) heat cramps. The cause and methods of preventing these are similar. However, the three conditions produce distinctive signs and symptoms-which everyone should be able to recognize at once in order to give proper care and attention to the victim.

(2) *Heat Stroke.* (a) *General.* This condition often appears suddenly. There is headache, dizziness, often with nausea and vomiting, and then collapse, delirium and unconsciousness. The first sign may be that of collapse. The important thing to remember is that *the skin is hot and dry.* This is due to the fact that in heat stroke the temperature goes very high (106° F. or higher).

(b) *Emergency treatment. The one thing that will save the victim's life is to lower his temperature quickly.* In the field do not wait for medical treatment or an ambulance, but immediately remove the patient's clothes except for the shorts, and whenever possible sprinkle his entire body with water. Have some attendants briskly rub the arms, and legs, and trunk to increase blood circulation to the skin and others fan him continually to increase the speed of water evaporation and its consequent cooling effect. Medical attention should be secured as soon as possible, as the patient will have to be hospitalized. However, measures to cool the body must be continued during the transfer of the patient to the hospital.

(3) *Heat exhaustion.* (a) *General.* This condition is manifested by headache, drowsiness, extreme weakness, dizziness and inability to walk. There may be some muscle cramps. The important thing to remember is that in *heat exhaustion the skin is moist, cold, and clammy.* While this condition is frequently incapacitating, the death rate is low.

(b) *Emergency treatment.* Removal of the individual to a cool place where he may rest and receive large quantities of salt water will usually bring about recovery. However, no chances must be taken, and medical attention must be secured or the patient hospitalized.

(4) *Heat cramps.* (a) *General.* Heat cramps are manifested by painful spasms of the muscles, more frequently of the legs, arms, and the abdominal wall. Their severity varies from mild and annoying to severe and completely disabling.

(b) *Emergency treatment.* These symptoms are directly due to lack of salt in the body. They are relieved when this salt loss is replaced. Treatment consists of drinking salt water freely. Severe cases must be hospitalized as it will probably be necessary to give the salt solution intravenously.

Mental and Psychological Training

The psychological effects of the jungle as outlined in paragraph 8 can be completely overcome only by experience, although common-sense talks are helpful. Training in jungle areas will do much to overcome these effects. In jungle warfare, as in all warfare, psychological and mental training to accustom the men's minds to the rigors of the battlefield are essential. The use of live ammunition and high explosives, overhead fire, and other phases of battlefield inoculation exercises are of increased importance in jungle warfare training because the jungle itself adds to the mental strain encountered in other battle areas. Extensive training of this type should be conducted in noncombat jungle areas.

Section II. REQUIREMENTS OF JUNGLE SERVICE

Discipline

An unusually high state of discipline is essential for successful jungle operations. Mental discipline, camouflage discipline, fire discipline, march discipline, light discipline—all phases of conduct must be guided by a strict sense of the effects of one's every action on the operation as a whole. Discipline in all its forms should be so thoroughly inculcated in the mind of each man that he not only conducts himself properly, but knows that each of the other men in the unit will do the same, under conditions of uncertainty and profound psychological strain. Strict enforcement of discipline by unit leaders is essential in all phases of jungle service.

Suspicion

The jungle fighter must be constantly suspicious. The high degree of concealment which the jungle offers requires slow and careful searching for the enemy; elements assigned security missions must search every possible hiding place to prevent the bypassing of enemy groups which might thereby be enabled to attack from the flanks or rear. There is always the possibility that enemy observers may be concealed nearby to discover and report preparations for a forthcoming operation. It is best to assume that the enemy is always nearby, watching and listening. The limited visibility of the jungle facilities deceptive tactics; adroit deception can frequently permit a small unit to overcome a force many times its own size. Ruses of many kinds may be applied. Demonstrations of strength in one area while attacking from another; ambushes; infiltration to attack command posts, supply points, and disrupt communications; and extensive use of snipers are forms of deceptive and harassing tactics which are well adapted to jungle terrain. It must be borne in mind that ruses are equally usable by the enemy, and constant care must be exercised not to fall a victim to deception. Important ruses must be initiated and coordinated by the largest unit involved in a particular operation.

Patience

One of the primary requisites of jungle operations is stealth. Stealthy movement requires patience. Similarly, patience is necessary to detect stealthy movement of the enemy. Patience, though not an American characteristic, can be learned and developed by constant practice. It is an essential of successful jungle operations.

Scouting and Patrolling

a. Small patrols of trained scouts will be able to move through jungle areas, avoid enemy outposts, slip through hostile defenses, and penetrate enemy rear areas. Such patrols will often constitute one of the most important means available to the commander for gaining information of the enemy.

b. Special training of members of such patrols should include jungle lore, training in concealment, movement, observation, knowledge of enemy characteristics and habits, and the identification of weapons by sound.

Leadership

The hardship of jungle operations demands the highest type of leadership. The difficulties of control necessitate decentralization, which results in increased importance of small-unit actions. Because of this, junior officers and noncommissioned officers must possess outstanding initiative, boldness, and determination. Similarly, the development of self-reliance on the part of each individual is an important training objective.

CHAPTER 2
LIVING IN THE JUNGLE

JUNGLE LORE

Jungle lore was taught to British and Indian troops in India in the training divisions and jungle warfare schools. For instance Lieutenant Colonel Jim Corbett, a jungle expert in tracking and killing man-eating tigers taught jungle lore around India. His book *Man-Eaters of Kumaon* was the recommended reading in the training divisions and translated into Roman Urdu. Similarly Captain Edgar Peacock, who had been a forest officer in Burma before the war, taught jungle lore at the jungle warfare schools, including the different uses of bamboo to make anything from bashas to cooking utensils (pp. 67–69).

The Jungle Lane to teach Jungle Lore
from *Army in India Training Memorandum No. 25*

1. The object of this jungle lane is to teach jungle lore, to show how nature can be used in the jungle, and to show our own and Jap methods of junglecraft.

2. The lane, which is an ordinary track running through the jungle, can be of any length, depending upon the amount of junglecraft and jungle lore is to be demonstrated. At the Jungle Warfare School, Shimoga, the lane is approximately 750 yards in length. The lane is made up of several demonstrations, which are shown one after the other. Each demonstration is then made the subject of a training period.

3. Points to be shown, are:—

(*a*) Correct use of light and shade and foliage, by patrols.

(*b*) Noise in close jungle.

(*c*) Sentries.

(*d*) Bird calls, cow bells, etc.

(*e*) Tree signs, Jap and our own.

(*f*) Booby traps, and bird snares. Grenades, panjis, spears, arrows, etc.

(*g*) Footprints.

(*h*) Leaves, and broken twigs.

(*i*) Snipers and false movement.

(*j*) Methods of cooking, Jap and our own.

(*k*) Shelters.

(*l*) Emplacements.

4. **Phase I.—Patrols**

(*a*) Bad. Patrol moving carelessly on track. Weapons not ready. Pulling on branches of bushes, etc. Sound heard and patrol halts on the track.

(*b*) Good. Patrol using both sides of the track inside the jungle. Silence, and rifles correctly held.

Note.—Explain to students that no patrol can be expected to get right up to a position without being seen, but a patrol can get near a position, before it is discovered.

5. **Phase II.—Noise**

(*a*) Chopping wood.

(*b*) Singing.

(*c*) Whistling.

(*d*) Laughter

(*e*) Combination of above.

Note.—Explain that this is a happy patrol going into harbour, and that they are giving themselves away by their noise. The result is:

(*f*) Jap attack signal. Gong.

(*g*) Jap attack.

Note.—The attack is made by two LMGs firing ball ammunition into a pit, and one machine carbine. Also four slabs of gun cotton. These are spread around the students, and just out of sight, to give the impression of being surrounded. Explain that noise of attack is made by three men only.

6. Phase III.—Sentries

(*a*) Lying,

(*b*) Sitting.

(*c*) Standing.

(*d*) Tree sentry.

Note.—Explain that these are sentries, and not snipers. They have a string or creeper attached from their post to the section commander.

One tug means a local, two tugs means an enemy, etc. Must be very patient, and silent, carefully concealed, and prepared to remain in the same position for hours.

7. Phase IV.—Calls

(*a*) Bird calls.

(*b*) Animal calls.

(*c*) Woodpecker.

(*d*) Frog.

(*e*) Cow bell.

Note.—Explain that men are very shy at first, and cannot make calls, etc., but if a competition is held, many calls will be forthcoming.

(*f*) Noise of woodpecker and frog, made with bamboo.

8. Phase V.—Tree signs

(*a*) Blazings on trees denoting passing of patrols, etc.

(*b*) Blazing, denoting hidden message.

(*c*) Arrow cut in ground.

(*d*) Bent branches and twigs.

(*e*) Jap method of marking night march.

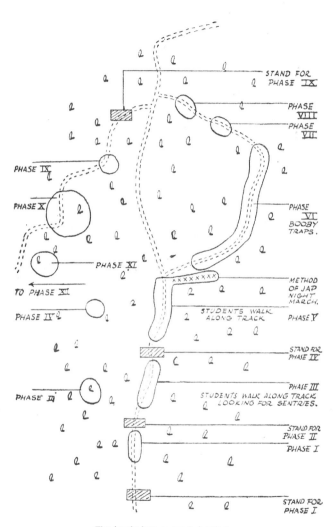

The jungle lane to teach jungle lore

(*f*) Methods of blocking a path.

(*g*) Cut wood on track denoting direction to be taken.

9. **Phase VI.—Booby traps**

(*a*) Panjis pit.

(*b*) Methods of using grenades.

(*c*) Note book on track.

(*d*) Rolled up shirt, containing grenade.

(*e*) Falling stone.

Note.—Explain that falling stone with a panji can be used for killing for meat.

(*f*) Flying arrow.

(*g*) Flying spear. Two kinds.

(*h*) Panjis lane.

(*i*) Bird snares.

10. **Phase VII.—Footprints**

(*a*) Boots. Ours and Jap.

Note.—Explain that Jap has got many of our boots, but has overnailed them.

(*b*) Shoes. Ours and Jap.

(*c*) Naked foot.

(*d*) Jap "tabi".

Note.—Explain that if footprints are not visible, can often be made so, by carefully blowing on the ground, when dust will go, leaving the impression behind.

11. **Phase VIII.—Leaves**

(*a*) Lane of teak leaves.

(*b*) Lane of jungle litter.

(*c*) Lane of dried bamboo leaf.

(*d*) Lane of broken twigs.

Note.—Walk over each lane in turn, and show that some leaves make more noise than others.

12. **Phase IX.—False movement**

Sniper fires, and at same time bush moves.

Note.—Explain that just before sniper fires, confederate pulls string attached to bush. Bush moves, and hence eye attracted to that direction.

13. **Phase X.—Cooking**

(*a*) Three stones.

(*b*) Two trenches.

(*c*) Horizontal bars with two forked sticks.

(*d*) Three pegs.

(*e*) Tin. Sand and petrol mixed.

(*f*) Sand pit.

(*g*) Pits cut in earth.

(*h*) Containers, made from bamboo.

Note.—Walls of bamboo should be shaved down to allow of quicker heating.

(*i*) Plates. Cups. Spoons.

(*j*) Headwear.

(*k*) Lighting fire, without matches, using bamboo-friction.

Note.—Explain that after food has been cooked all traces of area should be hidden, and no litter left behind.

14. **Phase XI.—Shelters**

(*a*) Lean-to. Made with one side only. Capable of taking three men.

(*b*) Lean-to. Made with two sides.

(*c*) Dog kennel.

Note.—Must have two exits.

(*d*) Raised floor. Usually used for a prolonged stay, such as in stockade.

Note.—Explain how long it takes to make each kind of shelter, and how many men are to be employed.

Explain that shelters will be made some distance away, and brought to present area. When patrol leaves area, shelters to be laid flat on the ground, so that Jap patrol cannot see from a distance.

15. **Phase XII.—Emplacements**

(*a*) MMG.

(*b*) Patrol shelter.

Note.—Explain that spoil must be removed to a distance. Connecting trenches to be covered over with branches, to prevent observation from the air.

Track discipline is essential.

Uses of Bamboo
from Military Training Pamphlet 52: *Warfare in the Far East*

(*a*) *Water container* (Fig 1). Cut a section of young bamboo and pierce a hole in the upper partition. After filling, close the hole with a roll of leaves. Use a strip of the outer bark as a loop for easy carriage.

(*b*) *Cooking container* (Fig 2).—The water container can be used for boiling water or cooking food. It will not burn out till the water is boiled or food cooked.

(*c*) *Cup* (Fig 3).

(*d*) *Plate* (Fig 4).

(*e*) *Spoon* (Fig 5).

(*f*) *Bamboo hnyis (hnis)* (Fig 6).—Split a narrow slip of bamboo longitudinally along the grain. Twist the strips for use as bindings and lashings as substitutes for rope or cord.

(*g*) *Bamboo mat* (Fig 7).—Cut a large bamboo into sections of the required length. Split them down on side. Cut out the partitions and make longitudinal cuts near rodes. Beat the sections flat. They may be used for the floors or walls of huts.

(*h*) *Bamboo raft* (Fig 8).—Size about 10 ft by 20 ft.

(i) Lash together, with cane or bamboo rope, three bundles of 15 to 20 bamboos each.

(ii) Lash transverse lengths of wooden poles to the bamboos, about 6 ft apart.

(iii) Place longitudinal lengths of wooden poles about 3 ft apart, and lash and notch them to the transverse poles.

(v) Tie down a row of bamboos across the transverse poles.

(vi) Spread and tie down split bamboo mattering on top.

(*i*) *Panjis* (Fig 9).—These are lengths of split bamboo, sharpened to needle points at once end and roughly pointed at the other. The sharp points may be fire hardened. They are made in all lengths and are set in the ground at an angle of 45 degrees. A man walking into a panji may be pierced in ankle, knee, thigh, or stomach. If he runs into one, he may be transfixed.

(*j*) *Frame for drying meat* (Fig 10).—Make a frame of four bamboo stakes driven into the ground. Place on the frame a lattice of split bamboos on which strips of meat can be hung. The meat should be dried out over a fire slowly and until quite hard.

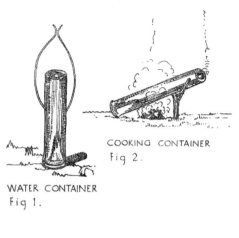

WATER CONTAINER
Fig 1.

COOKING CONTAINER
Fig 2.

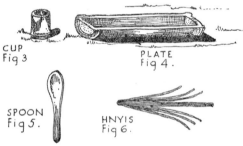

CUP
Fig 3

PLATE
Fig 4.

SPOON
Fig 5.

HNYIS
Fig 6.

(k) *Fire-making apparatus.*—Cut a length of dry bamboo about 10 ins long and split in half. Make a "V" shaped cut on the convex surface of the one half, taking care that the cut extends just a fraction into the concave side. Scrape some of the fine, inner skin from the bamboo, roll it into a tight ball, and place it directly under the cut to act as tinder. Place the bamboo, convex side uppermost, flat on the ground, and hold it in place with your feet. Shape a length of dry bamboo to fit the cut; place it in the cut; grasp both ends firmly and, applying plenty of pressure, rub it backwards and forwards through the

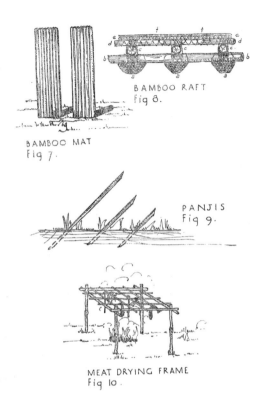

BAMBOO MAT
Fig 7.

BAMBOO RAFT
Fig 8.

PANJIS
Fig 9.

MEAT DRYING FRAME
Fig 10.

cut as fast as possible. The tinder under the cut will soon catch fire and can be blown into a flame. Similarly a magnifying glass or the lens of a pair of spectacles may be used with the sun's rays to ignite tinder. Another quick method is to extract the bullet from a cartridge, replace it with dry rag, cotton, or tinder, and fire the cartridge on the ground. The material used should catch fire and smoulder.

FOOD

Rations in the jungle were monotonous and did little to restore energy to men continually exerting themselves. For example during Operation Longcloth, the first Chindit campaign, the staple ration consisted of 12oz Shakapura biscuit, 2oz cheese, 1 oz milk powder, 9oz raisins and almonds, 4oz sugar, a tiny allowance of acid drops or chocolate, salt which was all washed down with mugs of tea and accompanied by the inevitable cigarettes. The deficiency of these rations led to the adoption of new US food packs for Operation Thursday, the second Chindit operation, called the K ration. Each daily K ration of three packs marked breakfast, dinner and supper, all of which could be eaten hot or cold. Breakfast consisted of instant coffee, powdered milk, a tin of cheese flecked with ham, biscuits, sugar and date bar. The dinner pack comprised lemonade powder, tinned spam, biscuits, chocolate and a fruit bar. Supper was similar fare, with soup powder replacing the lemonade. Four cigarettes were included in each pack, as well as toilet paper. The dearth of tea proved a major sticking point for British soldiers on campaign, however, and tea, powdered milk and sugar were issued as a supplement. The initial appeal of K rations to British troops quickly disappeared. By the end of the 1944 campaign the K ration was universally hated. The most serious drawback was that they were simply inadequate for the task with insufficient calories for the men.

Rations were supplemented by supply drops delivering fresh rations and could be supplemented by food available in the jungle , and the Allies brought together information to enable men to safely add to the variety and quantity of their rations from local food sources. As reported in *Tactical and Technical Trends* in 1943, an American team undertook an expedition to test whether sufficient food could be found (see pp. 73–75). In England the Biology War Committee produced an illustrated pamphlet, *Living in the Jungle,* which stated its aim as 'to help you fend for yourself in the jungle….The hints and warning given should not by any means by taken lightly.' However none of the Allied material comes close to a recommendation in the Japanese pamphlet for troops going overseas: 'If poisonous snakes are found they must be killed. The liver can be taken (as a medicine) and the flesh roasted and eaten (as food). There is no better tonic than this.'

The provision of drinking water remained a problem. Quite often troops operated in arid areas with a real lack of water and strict water discipline was enforced as a result, though water could be plentiful in some jungle areas (see pp. 76–77).

Military Training Pamphlet No. 9 (India)
The Jungle Book

XIII. ADMINISTRATION.

3. Ration Scales.—There are, at present, five different scales of rations for British and Indian troops, *viz.*—

(a) Normal field service scales, "A" for British troops and "C" for Indian troops.

(b) Compo-pack (8 men), separate packs, non cooking scales "B" for British troops and "D" for Indian troops.

(c) 48 hour Mess Tin Ration, the same for British troops and Indian troops.

(d) Light Scale Ration, the same for British troops and Indian troops.

(e) Emergency Ration.

There is no "hard scale" ration. When it is necessary to travel light the scale given at (d) is used.

The gross weights of the various types of rations are:—

F. S. Scale British troops (gross) 5 lbs. 13ozs. (exclusive of cigarettes, matches and fuel.)

F. S. Scale Indian troops (gross) 3 lbs. 14 ozs. (exclusive of cigarettes, matches and fuel.)

Compo-pack British troops (8 men)	30 lbs. 12 ozs.
Compo-pack Indian troops (8 men)	31 lbs. 4 ozs.
48 hours Mess Tin Ration	1 lb. 8½ ozs.
Light Scale Ration	2 lbs.
Emergency Ration	1 lb. (inclusive of the ration tin).

Whenever possible men will be issued with the normal F. S. Scale.

4. The Compo-pack.—This is a non-cooking ration which can be issued on all occasions when it is not possible to provide the F. S. Scale.

The eight rations are packed in a standard 4 gal. kerosene tin. This pack is convenient for dropping from the air.

To provide variety, there are six different types of British troop packs.

For Indian troops there is only type of compo-pack.

5. The 48 hour Mess Tin Ration.—The use of this ration is limited to 48 hours and it is intended for issue to assault troops only. Being a universal ration it contains no cigarettes or matches. The rations are packed in two craft paper packs and then placed in 4 gals. type kerosene tins.

6. The Light Scale.—This ration is packed similarly to the 48 hour Mess Tin Ration but in a 24 hour pack; each 4 gal. tin holding ten rations.

Normally the scale will NOT be issued for periods exceeding SIX in any consecutive TWENTY days. Should, however, it be found necessary to employ this scale for a longer period, it will be supplemented with other items selected from those comprising the F. S. scales, or by dehydrated meat and vegetables.

7. The Emergency Ration.—This ration is packed in a sealed tin. It is carried on the man and is only intended to cover a period of 24 hours.

8. Reserve Rations.—To enable a unit to be independent of daily ration deliveries, reserve rations may often have to be carried. A suitable reserve consists of three day's light rations. The decision to operate independently of ration deliveries is, however, not one to be taken lightly, since the increase in weight on the man means a corresponding decrease in his fighting efficiency. Whether it must be clearly recognised that there is not the same nutritive value in non-cooking rations as there is in the Field Service Scale. Troops cannot therefore be expected to operate for long periods on non-cooking or light scales of rations without a loss of physical efficiency which will not be apparent until the troops are already suffering seriously from mal-nutrition.

Food available in the Jungle
from *Tactical and Technical Trends* 21

Eight noncommissioned officers of the 1st Battalion and myself accompanied two French officers and two platoons of the New Hebrides Defense Forces (native troops), on a 4-day reconnaissance trip up the Teouma River. The primary purpose of the trip was to see if it were possible for 75 to 100 men to live off the land indefinitely in the jungles of this island.

Although 3 days' rations were carried by each man, very little was touched except tea and biscuits. It was conclusively proved to my satisfaction that men who are resourceful and who will take the time to learn a little jungle lore can easily live and thrive healthfully in these jungles all about us.

a. Types of Food

To list by group all the various foods we found in the jungle:

Meats
Wild chicken
Wild duck
Wild pigeon
Wild cattle
Wild pig
Flying fox
Fish (mullet)
Eel
Fresh water crayfish (prawn)

Vegetables (all year round)
Taro
Yam
Manioc
Hearts of palm trees
Hearts of pandamus

Nuts
Coconut (all year round)
Navele (September, October)

Fruits
Bananas (all year round)
Oranges (May, June, July)
Tangerines (May, June, July)
Lemons (May, June, July)
Bread fruit (February, March)
Wild raspberries (September, October)
Nakarika (October, November)
Papaya (all year round)
Mangoes (October, February)

Water vine

b. Poisonous Vegetation

We learned that there were seven varieties of nangalat, a poisonous leaf that upon contact with human flesh produces an instantaneous burning sensation and itching that lasts usually about 1 week. The native remedy is to rub immediately the juice from the stem of the poisonous nagalat (the same one that touched you) on the affected part. The worst variety of nangalat can be recognized by the red veins running all through the leaves and by the escalloped edges of the leaves. There is also a poison tree called the "goudron," which is easily distinguished by its coal black sap which invariably runs profusely down some part of the trunk. If you sleep under this tree, you will be taken sick and suffer with a severe headache lasting a long time. If you cut into the tree or in any way contact the "black blood" (as the natives call it), you may get a severe poisoning which puffs up the skin of the face and hands with a very dangerous and painful rash. Once subjected to this poisoning, one need only approach within 50 feet of a "goudron" tree to get the same poisoning all over again. Some people have been known to have been so severely poisoned that they never were completely well again.

c. Lumber Products

We learned that the bark of the rotin (rattan) tree (the wood that all the fences around us are made of) makes a rope of any desired size. It is practically impossible to break even a fine thread of it. The bourée tree is also excellent for this purpose.

We learned to recognize several very hard woods that are excellent for building anything you wish to last for a long time.

There is a very common bush all about us from which is extracted ricin oil; it is used to produce a high-grade aviation oil.

d. Methods of Cooking

An interesting thing was to see how the native troops cooked the fish, prawn (crayfish), and meat that we ate. There were two methods used in cooking the fish. The first method was to clean and scale the fish, and then wrap them up in wild banana leaves. The bundle was then tied securely with rotin-bark twine, placed on a hastily constructed wood griddle, and roasted thoroughly until done. The second method was to wrap up the fish in the same manner, and then place the bundle well down inside and underneath a pile of stones which had been heated in advance until they were red hot.

The crawfish were dumped alive into a hollow section of bamboo about 2 feet long, and thus roasted over the open fire. The bamboo chars, but does not burn through. They were very delicious. Meat was cut into small chunks and packed down into this same type of bamboo roasting stick. Meat cooked this way would last from 3 to 4 days without spoiling, if left inside the bamboo stick with the ends sealed. The meat for immediate consumption was cut into steaks and roasted on sticks much as we would roast "hot dogs."

Yam, taro, manioc, and wild bananas were cooked in the coals, and tasted not unlike potatoes if you stretched your imagination a little. Hearts of palm made a refreshing salad, and papaya a delicious dessert.

All the wild meat was gamey, and generally a little tough. However, it tasted mighty good after a long march.

<u>e. Methods of Fishing</u>

The natives used two methods of fishing. If a large quantity of fish is desired, they seek out a good deep pool where fish are in considerable numbers, and toss in a hand grenade. This usually yields anywhere from 20 to 60 fish. The largest were around 15 inches long. If a few fish were desired, the natives would scrape a little bark from a navele tree, wrap it up in a leaf, and, wading with the leaf in one hand and a machete in another, drop it over a pool of fish or even a single fish. The curious fish would swim up to the leaf, and, when they did, the juice from the bark of the navele tree would knock them "groggy," and they would float up to the surface in a daze, easy prey for a machete.

<u>f. Shelter</u>

The natives would construct a combination bed and shelter against the rain in about 15 minutes. The bed was built about 3 feet above the ground by laying stout but pliable reeds over a framework supported by forked stakes. Several layers of large, fine ferns were then put on, thus forming a very comfortable bed. Another series of longer, forked stakes were placed alongside the short ones to support a food about 6 feet above the ground. The roof was constructed in the same manner as the bed.

Drinking water from the Rattan Vine
from *Tactical and Technical Trends* 34

a. General

Officers returning from the S. W. Pacific area report that good drinking water is hard to find in the jungle. A source of excellent water exists in many jungle areas in the shape of the rattan vine, from which a copious water-supply may be drawn by cutting off a section of the vine and allowing the water to run out of the severed section into a canteen cup. While the fact that this vine will supply water, together with a description of the rattan palm-vine, appeared in Technical Training Manual 10-420*, page 16, a more complete description of the plant and its potentiality as a supplier of good drinking water appears to be desirable. The information upon which this account is based was furnished through the courtesy of Dr. E. H. Walker of the Smithsonian Institution and Dr. E. D. Merrill, Director of the Arnold Arboretum, Harvard University.

b. A Word of Caution

While other tropical vines produce drinkable water, and possibly sap from most vines that <u>do not produce a milky juice</u> may be drunk in extreme emergency, they are not to be recommended <u>unless used by local natives</u>. All rattans, however, are safe, and while the rattan vine-palm is usually found in the higher jungles, it occurs also in coastal jungles where most of our forces are now operation.

c. The Rattan Palm

There are many different kinds of rattan palm; all are climbing palms, with vine-like characteristics, see sketch. It will be noted that out of the tips of the palm leaves, the central stem is prolonged into a vine which may be from 100 to 250 feet long, and vary in thickness from the diameter of a pencil to 2½ inches. These vines, as many a soldier knows to his sorrow, are supplied with very sharp, hard, claw-like teeth similar to rose thorns, growing out of their shoots or tendrils, or from the leaf stems. Incidentally, the lower foot or two of the trunk of the palm contains some starch. These lower parts, which are slightly thickened, may be roasted and the baked starch "chewed out." Rattan vines may run along the ground or climb high on jungle trees. Those found low and in the shade give a cooler water than the vines exposed to hot sunlight.

d. How To Tap the Vine

To tap the vine, chop off a thick section from two to eight feet long, making the upper cut first. Never make the lower cut first. Hold the cut segment, butt end down over a canteen cup, when the sap will begin to drip or flow out. When the flow ceases, cut off a foot or more from the top end, more water will trickle out. This process may be repeated until there is no more water left in the stem.

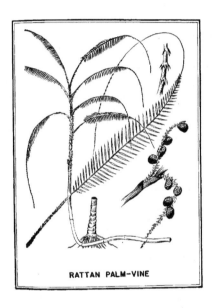

RATTAN PALM-VINE

Field Manual 72-20: *Jungle Warfare*
Appendix I: Native Plants

1. General

Wild fruits, nuts, and edible plants exist in great number and variety throughout jungle areas. Personnel operating in such areas should make every effort to learn to identify these, as well as the relatively few poisonous ones. This may be done by making field trips, talking to natives, and visiting botanical gardens and museums (see pars. 4 and 7).

2. Poisonous Plants

a. GENERAL. Poisonous plants are of three kinds: those whose fruit, nuts or portions of the plant itself are poisonous if eaten, for example, the physic nut (see fig. 11); those whose juice is a contact poison; and those which produce a mechanical "poison" or sting. A plant which is particularly dangerous if the juice enters the blood stream is strychnos (see fig. 12) from which the deadly curare poison is extracted by certain primitive peoples of tropical America. Methods of distinguishing poisonous fruits and nuts from the nonpoisonous are described in paragraphs 4, 6, and 7.

Figure 11. Physic nut. A shrub common in hedges throughout the southwest Pacific area. The large seeds are violently poisonous, and should not be eaten under any circumstances.

Figure 12. Strychnos. A slender, woody vine, easily recognizable by the small hairs on all parts. The fruit is shaped like a ball, and usually is 2 inches or more in diameter, with a hard green or yellow skin. It holds several large seeds. In some parts of Brazil it is called "Urari." The bark and roots are a source of "curare" one of the deadliest poisons known. A small quantity in the blood stream will paralyze the nerves almost instantly, and soon cause death. It has been used by the South American Indians for poisoning arrows and the darts from blow guns. It is reported that similar use of the plant is made by the Indians of Panama.

Figure 13. Manzanillo. A small tree common on seashores in many parts of tropical America, and abundant on both coasts of Panama, where it forms dense thickets along the beaches. The bark is smooth and pale brown; the leaves are small, smooth and green. The flowers are green, and are arranged in stiff spikes. The fruit is over an inch in diameter, and resembles a small green apple. The fruit is poisonous. The milky sap is highly irritating, like the juice of poison ivy. Smoke from the burning wood may cause irritation to the eyes.

Figure 14. Nettle. (Ortiga in Spanish). The nettle is found in many parts of the world. That variety known in Spanish as the ortiga, is common on the Pacific slope of Paguma, particularly in dry regions along the beaches. It grows about 3 to 5 feet high. It is covered with stiff hairs which, when they sting the flesh, cause great pain which often lasts for a day or longer, and is sometimes accompanied by high fever. The flowers are white, and about ½ inch in diameter.

b. CONTACT POISONS. If a man has become exposed to a plant whose juice is a contact poison, he should promptly wash the exposed parts of his body with water and issue soap. Local inhabitants can often furnish information making it possible to identify plants which are dangerous or annoying in this respect. An example is the manzanillo, found in tropical America and illustrated in figure 13.

c. STINGING PLANTS. Certain types of plants with stingy hairs on their surfaces produce a mechanical irritant, frequently highly painful and in certain cases, if the hairs are taken into the intestinal tract or mucous membranes, dangerous. Examples are the cowitch and the nettle. One variety of the latter found in tropical America is the ortiga (see fig. 14).

3. Native Use of Plants

In all parts of the region the inhabitants in general know both the wild and the cultivated plants which may be used as food. However, the use of a certain species of plant as food may be common in one area, but quite uncommon in other areas. For example, the breadfruit, which is a basic food in many parts of Polynesia, is little used as food in most parts of Malaya, where the species also occurs, simply because better foods are usually available there.

4. Advice of Natives
Whenever possible, one should try to get in touch with natives even though one may be able to talk with them only by means of signs. They can be most helpful in times when regular rations are not available. They usually know how these emergency food plants should be prepared, and which may be poisonous if eaten raw. In some of the actually poisonous plants, the poisonous elements may be eliminated by proper cooking or by other treatment after which the material may be eaten with safety.

5. Local Names
In jungle areas, there are many different languages and dialects used. For all plants of this vast region there are probably in excess of 50,000 native plant names actually recorded; many locally used plant names are still unlisted. Some native plant names are very widely used, while others are local. Many of the plants have no English names.

6. Guide for Eating Fruits
Cultivated trees and shrubs growing in and near the settled areas and bearing attractive fleshy fruits, for the most part are actually planted for their fruits, which generally may be eaten with perfect safety. In the wild, where monkeys occur, a general safeguard to follow is to observe what the monkeys actually eat in the form of wild fruits. The feeding habits of birds is not such a safe guide. One should keep in mind constantly that fruit maturity in the tropics is normally seasonal, just as it is in temperate regions, and only occasionally, as with the coconut palm, are fruits produced throughout the year.

7. Edible Plants
a. For a detailed study of edible plants, see TM 10-420.

b. The food plants described and illustrated in the pages which follow were selected on the basis of their abundance and their simplicity of preparation for eating, as well as the comparative ease with which they may be recognized. Many others exist, some of them as widespread as the examples shown. Soldiers should make every effort to learn first-hand of edible plants in the particular locality where they are stationed. Positive identification can be learned only by first-hand knowledge of the plants. Study in botanical gardens and museums will help. Field trips, preferably under the guidance of informed friendly native inhabitants, are the best means of learning plant identification.

 c. In addition to the edible plants listed herein, many of the familiar garden vegetables such as cabbage, beets, corn, beans, squash, cucumber, and egg plant are cultivated by natives. Fruits such as bananas, pineapples, lemons, oranges, and limes are also found. These are not shown on the following pages because of the average man's familiarity with their appearance. It must be remembered that cultivated fruits and vegetables belong to some native inhabitant, and must not be picked except by permission of the owner. Few natives would object to an individual soldier's picking a small quantity of his crop, particularly if the soldier is separated from his unit and is obviously taking the food as an emergency measure. However, the presence of cultivated plants is an indication of nearby habitation where food, shelter, medical aid, and assistance in regaining contact with one's unit can usually be obtained, and it might be more desirable to find the nearby native village early, rather than to stop and eat from a man's garden.

Figure 15. Akee (Huevo vegetal in Spanish). A small tree with double leaves. The fruit has three cells, and is colored red or orange. It contains three large black shiny seeds each seated in a white center. The center is the edible part of the fruit. It is usually boiled in salt water, and then fried, but can be eaten raw. The SEEDS and the UNRIPE FRUIT which has not opened by itself on the tree, are POISONOUS.

Figure 16. Bamboo shoot. Bamboo, familiar to almost everyone, is found throughout tropical Asia and the Pacific Islands. The young shoots, up to a foot or so in height, can be eaten raw, but are much more palatable when cooked. In addition to use as food, bamboo provides material for the construction of many expedient tools and receptacles.

Figure 17. Black palm. A tree with very hard black wood. The meat around the orange or red fruits is sweet, and although stringy can be eaten (raw only).

Figure 18. Breadfruit (Fruita de Pan in Spanish). A large tree 20 to 40 feet high, a native of the East Indies, and now found throughout Polynesia, as well as in the West Indies and Panama. The leaves are large, sharply lobed, dark, and glossy, and have a sticky, milky juice. The fruit is from 6 to 10 inches in diameter, round or oval in shape, and has a rough, yellowish green surface. It may be eaten when thoroughly cooked by baking, and although extremely dry is a good substitute for potatoes.

Figure 19. Cashew (Marañon in Spanish). A tree growing as high as 30 feet, found in fields and on the sides of high bushy hills in Central America. The leaves are leathery, and are yellowish-green in color; the flowers are pink. The fruit consists of a large grayish, kidney-shaped nut hanging from a red or yellow, spongy juicy mass about the size and shape of a pepper. The pepper-shaped mass can be eaten raw. The nut can be eaten after it has been roasted until all the oil evaporates; otherwise it is poisonous. The oil in the nut should not be touched with the bare hands, as it irritates the skin, and causes swelling.

Figure 20. Coconut (Coco or Cocotero in Spanish). The coconut, found in tropical regions throughout the world, usually grows in flat areas along the banks of streams or on the coast. The tree grows as high as 100 feet, with large green or brownish fronds often 20 feet long. The nuts grow in clusters at the base of the fronds. The meat of both green and ripe nuts is edible, although that of the former is by far the more digestible. The water or "milk" of the green nut is very palatable, and is frequently a satisfactory substitute for water. In order to extract the water or meat of the nut, the large outer husk must either be stripped or cut away. A stout stake with a sharp point, buried in the ground at an angle is useful in husking.

Figure 21. Grape. Wild grapes are, in general, confined to the temperate zone, however there is one which is native to Central America and is known as the Uva or Bejuco de Agua. This variety is common in thickets about Panama. The fruit is very small and sour, but the stem contains a large amount of sap which is a safe substitute for water.

Figure 22. Guava. A native of tropical America, now widely distributed throughout Malaysia and Polynesia, particularly in open areas. The tree is from 6 to 20 feet high, and has short stalked leaves with strongly marked veins, and covered with a soft down. The fruit is pear shaped, about the size of a hen's egg, and covered with a thin bright yellow skin filled with a many-seeded soft pulp. This last is yellow, pink, or red in color, has a pleasant sweet-acid aromatic flavor, and is eaten raw. Jelly and paste are made from the boiled fruit.

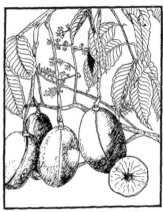

Figure 23. Hog plum (Circuelo in Spanish). A small tree, very common in Panama, both in open fields or on bushy hillsides. The fruit, which can be eaten raw or cooked, resembles a plum, and is usually red or orange.

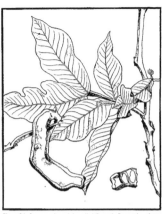

Figure 24. Ice cream bean (also called Guava in Panama). A tree common in Central America. The leaves are hairy, dark green on top, and light green underneath. The fruit, which can be eaten raw only, looks like a bean, and has a thick, sweet, juicy pulp, containing seeds.

Figure 25. Mango. The mango is common in Malaysia, Polynesia, and tropical America, usually in a cultivated state, although a few wild ones may be found. The tree is usually large and spreading, with smooth, dark green glossy leaves. The fruit is 2 to 6 inches long, and is green, yellow or orange red when ripe, according to the variety. Some mangoes have a strong turpentine taste, but are safe to eat. If not peeled before being eaten, the juice of the skin, particularly at the base of the stem, may cause a skin rash, particularly around the mouth, which develops into "mango sores." The sap of some of the wild species of mango trees found in Malaya, all with edible fruit, has a very irritating effect upon the skin, like that of poison ivy. Mangos are generally eaten raw, but may be cooked.

Figure 26. Papaya. Found throughout the Pacific Islands and in Panama. The tree has a single straight, grayish trunk from 6 to 20 feet high, with a cluster of long-stalked uneven-edged leaves at the top. The trunk is pulpy and brittle, and can be cut through with one or two blows of a machete. The fruit resembles a muskmelon in appearance, is green or yellow when ripe, and contains many black shot-like seeds in the interior cavity. The skin of the fruit and the tree itself exude a milky sap which may cause skin irritation. Ripe papayas are eaten raw, but green ones should be cooked by boiling. The sap will make meat tender if placed on it before cooking, or in the water if the meat is being boiled.

Figure 27. Polynesian chestnut. A small to medium-sized tree found in Polynesia, and as a larger tree in Malaysia and tropical Asia. The nuts, which are eaten either boiled or roasted, grow in large pods, each containing a single seed or nut. They are well-flavored and highly nutritious.

Figure 28. Sapodilla or Nispero. A large tree, growing as high as 60 feet, found in tropical America. The leaves are shiny and dark green. The fruit, about 2 inches in diameter, is ball-shaped, with thin brown skin which may be either scaly or smooth. It is eaten raw only.

Figure 29. Soursop (Guanabana in Spanish). A small tree of tropical America, with smooth, dark-green leaves which are strongly scented when crushed. The spiny fruits are often as large as a man's head, and weigh up to 10 or 12 pounds. The juicy white pulp, crushed and with water added, makes a palatable beverage. This pulp can also be eaten raw.

Figure 30. Star apple (Caimito in Spanish). A common tropical American forest tree which grows as high as 60 feet. The leaves are dark green on top, and have shiny silky brown hairs on the bottom. The fruit, which has a smooth green or purple skin, resembles a small apple in appearance. The fruit, which has a sweet, greenish milky meal, is eaten raw only. When the fruit is cross cut through the center, the brown seeds make a star-shaped figure.

Figure 31. Taro (Badu in Central America). The taro, or badu is widely cultivated in Oceania and Malaysia and is also cultivated in Central America. It is grown in swampy and, less commonly, in upland areas. The plant is 2 to 3 feet high, and has leaves closely resembling those of the larger, and inedible "elephant ears" which are grown as ornamental plants in the United States as well as in the tropics. Taro has thick hairy tubers somewhat larger than potatoes. The tubers, as well as the young leaves, are edible, but all must be thoroughly cooked, preferably by boiling. "Poi," a staple food in many parts of the Pacific, is made by pounding and kneading the peeled boiled tuber, adding water and allowing the resulting paste to ferment slightly. It is very palatable to those who become accustomed to it.

Figure 32. Water chestnut (Fruita de Mono in Spanish). A small or medium-sized tree growing in wet forests or swamps in tropical America. Only a few branches grow out from the trunk. The shiny green leaves have 5 to 7 narrow leaflets, usually pointed at the tip. The large flowers are a pinkish color. The fruit is reddish brown and about 8 to 10 inches long. It is very hard and heavy, and the brown seeds are imbedded in solid white flesh. The large seeds are eaten raw, or roasted and eaten like chestnuts.

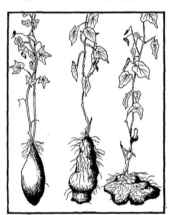

Figure 33. Yam. A plant found in both a wild and cultivated state throughout the south Pacific and in tropical America. The stems are long, usually twining, reddish-green in color, and have numerous small flowers. The tuber resembles the sweet potato, but is usually larger, sometimes weighing as much as 40 pounds. The skin is rough and brown; the meat white to purplish. One variety of yam, with a leaf made up of 3 leaflets with somewhat spiny stems, is poisonous unless properly prepared, and should be avoided. The edible varieties have either a single leaf, or a leaf made up of 5 leaflets. Yams must be cooked before eating, either boiled or roasted in the same manner as a sweet potato.

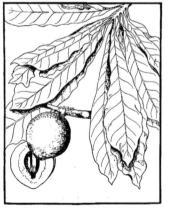

Figure 34. Zapote. A large tree of tropical America sometimes growing to a height of 100 feet. The leaves, pale green on top and paler underneath, are 6 to 12 inches long. The fruit is ball-shaped, 4 to 8 inches in diameter, with rough, brownish skin and pink or reddish meat in which are several large shiny brown seeds. It is usually eaten raw, but may be eaten cooked.

GUYS THAT DESERVE EVERY CREDIT HERE — LITTLE BEARERS ON A JUNGLE TRAIL AT THE FRONT — THEY'RE UNDER SNIPER FIRE, TOO & FEW ARE ARMED

SGT HOWARD BRODIE GUADALCANAL

MEDICAL

Disease, and malaria in particular, caused many casualties for troops fighting in the jungle. By 1943 medical advances meant that malaria could be contained through insecticides, anti-malarial discipline and medicines, including mepracrine. Anti-malarial discipline was strictly enforced with commanding officers being sacked if they didn't enforce it. For example, all tents and shelters were sprayed before morning and evening parades and all men had to apply anti-mosquito cream. Malaria casualties in forward areas were now treated at the Malarial Forward Treatment Units and thus the unit and lines of communication were less affected by malaria casualties. By March 1944 only two out of 100 SWPA personnel were in hospital at any given time with an average stay in hospital of nine days.

Medical Problems in Jungle Warfare and The Pacific Area Command and General Staff School

1. IMPORTANCE.—

Lack of prior planning and careful study of sanitary and medical problems may mean failure to any force attempting Jungle Operations.

Because of the increasing importance of this problem the following information has been extracted partially from FM 31-20 and largely from recent reports from certain Theaters of Operations.

2. HIGH PHYSICAL STANDARDS.—

The Jungle task force should be especially selected as to physical fitness, and should comprise very young men who can withstand the hardships of this exhausting service. Unfit, physically weak and elderly personnel should be eliminated before this special military operation is undertaken. Our troops on Bataan were amazed at the extremely youthful appearance of Japanese prisoners.

3. SPECIAL TRAINING FOR JUNGLE WARFARE.—

Very important for all the force—including attached units, especially medical troops. A few weeks are considered necessary to acclimatize troops to increased temperatures, rains, humidity, the peculiar noises, etc., incident to the tropics. As a further hardening process, a number of weeks additional training under actual jungle conditions should be carried on before troops are ready for such operations. Litter bearers should also train in the jungle to be able to carry loaded litters long distances over trails. Combat troops do not enjoy littering the litter-bearers, as sometimes happens. Pack animals should be conditioned with loads out on hilly jungle trails in order to be fit.

4. VACCINATION.—

Should be accomplished as prescribed by Army Regulations and War Department Circulars; they must be carefully checked to determine if all the troops have complied. This should be done by medical officers prior to departure of the Task Force.

5. PERSONAL HYGIENE.—

a. Dehydration—In the jungle where the humidity is high, sweat does not evaporate but runs off the body; therefore, cooling is less efficient and water losses are greater. The loss of water through sweat is associated with a loss of salt. If this water is not replaced physical efficiency is soon lost, and later heat exhaustion will develop. The lost salt must be replaced along with the water, or muscular cramps of the abdomen and extremities will develop. Troops should be encouraged to take the maximum amount of salt with their food, (under jungle conditions this will not cause increased thirst because salt increases thirst only when there is an excess of it) and required to take it with all drinking water. A 1/10% solution is well tolerated and after a short period the taste is not objectionable.

b. Water Discipline—Strict water discipline should be enforced at all times. Water discipline consists of drinking only purified water to which 1/10 per cent salt has been added (1/4 teaspoonful or 2 ten grain tablets to each canteen of water). Soldiers should drink as their thirst requires and take enough to satisfy thirst. A large quantity of cold water should not be drunk while the soldier is hot as it may cause stomach cramps. It is better to drink slower— "by the numbers." Two Halazone (chlorine) tablets to a canteenful of water, with 30-minute contact period, will sterilize water for drinking.

c. Chilling—In some areas of the jungle there may be some danger of men becoming chilled at night if they sleep on wet ground. When the heat is not sufficient for sweating to continue throughout the night, the men should strip and put on dry clothing including socks. This will prevent chilling and thus lower the incidence of respiratory diseases. In addition the skin will be kept dry thereby reducing skin irritation and infection. Where possible, the jungle hammock should be used for sleeping. (It may be suspended in a slit trench.) When this is not feasible, use a bedding of leaves or grass covered with shelter half. During the rainy season, erect shelter tent over a small platform ("wikiup"), in order to sleep off the wet ground and keep dry. A poncho is useful.

d. Ability to swim.—Every man should be able to swim, as there are many streams to be crossed in the jungle, and drownings are not uncommon.

e. Feet and skin—The best preventative of all jungle foot infections is to keep the feet dry as much of the time as possible. The feet should be washed with soap and water daily, preferably at night; thoroughly dried and lightly dusted with powder. Clean socks should be worn at all times, changing daily if dry socks are available. Excessive use of foot powder may cause maceration of the skin as it soon becomes wet with sweat and forms a sticky mass between the toes.

Surf bathing is usually satisfactory, but bathing, swimming or wading in some inland waters is dangerous because they may contain *schistosomes*, a parasite that will invade the body tissues through the skin causing disease.

When bathing facilities are not available, a brisk rubbing with a towel while the body is wet with sweat will clean it. A small amount of soap on a wet cloth should be used to sponge arm pits and groin, followed by a rinse of clean water. Frequent foot and skin inspections are desirable, as skin infections may rank SECOND ONLY TO MALARIA as a cause of noneffectiveness.

6. MALARIA.—
The greatest cause of noneffectiveness of military personnel in Jungle Operations.

Following is a condensation of sanitary and preventive measures for malaria control in effect in one of our Theaters of Operations.

   a. Prior to movement of a command into a malarious area:

   (1) Sanitary survey to determine the probable effect of conditions or sickness rate of troops and prevalence of malaria and other insect or waterborne diseases. Where the military situation permits, specially trained medical personnel will be dispatched in advance of troops to make a health survey of the area, and submit recommendations.

   (2) A medical officer especially qualified in tropical diseases will be attached to commander's staff to advise on relative malaria hazards of various proposed camp and bivouac sites and to supervise anti-malaria work and discipline. Malaria survey and control units will be attached when tactical operations permit, and the Malariologist will be used to the fullest.

   (3) Commanding officers will form and train anti-malarial details in each company, squadron, or smaller unit. Detail made up of one NCO and two enlisted men per infantry company and a proportionate number for each smaller unit or detachment. Routine anti-malaria work in each unit area will be done by these details, augmented as necessary. Unit commander will be responsible for anti-malaria work as advised by the attached medical officer.

   (4) Military personnel will be thoroughly trained before departure in effecting anti-malaria measures.

   (5) Each individual's equipment will include the following anti-malaria supplies and equipment:

      Bar, mosquito, or hammock, jungle complete.

Headnet, mosquito.

Gloves, mosquito.

Repellent, mosquito—2oz. bottle.

Atabrine, 30 tablets, 0.1 gm (1½ grains each).

(6) Each organization will be issued the following one month's maintenance stocks:

Bars, mosquito—25 per 100 men.

Headnets, mosquito—10 per 100 men.

Gloves, mosquito—10 prs per 100 men.

Repellent, mosquito—400 2-oz. bottles per 100 men.

Atabrine, tablets—0.1 gm—(1½ grains) 3,000 tablets per 100 men for suppressive treatment.

Insecticide, aerosol—1 lb. dispenser, 300 per 1,000 men.

Equipment:

Sprayer, hand, insecticide—10 per each 100 men.

Sprayer, knapsack type—1 per each 200 or less men.

Malariol (or Diesel Oil No. 2)—1 drum 50 gallon US per sprayer knapsack.

Insecticide, for use in hand sprayers—5 gallons US per 100 men.

Unit anti-malarial supplies will be conspicuously marked and carried in a readily *accessible place on the ship*, to be available immediately upon arrival. (Combat Loading)

b. Anti-malaria measures for military personnel in malarious areas:

(1) Unit commanders will be responsible for enforcement of anti-malaria measures in their commands. Medical officers will give regular instruction in malaria control measures as well as other phases of hygiene and sanitation.

(2) (a) *Suppressive treatment* may be initiated on the advice of the Medical Department when troops are being sent to a malarious area. No blanket rule can be laid down; in general, suppressive treatment should be used where mosquito control measures do not afford adequate protection against malaria. The taking of one Atabrine tablet (0.1gm) once daily with a drink of water at meal time, seven days a week, has been found effective. The skin may show some yellow discoloration, which disappears in time. Suppressive treatment will be supervised by a *commissioned officer* in order to insure that *each soldier actually* swallows the medication.

(b) *Method of Administering Atabrine to Troops in Ranks:*

(i) *Personnel Per Platoon:* 1 Commissioned Officer; 1 NCO and 2 Enlisted Men.

(ii) *Duties:* (As specified below.)

(iii) *Equipment:*

Supply of Water (in Lyster Bag).

2 small tables (or 1 Table 12 feet long); may use substitute in combat.

Roster of the Company (Platoon), alphabetically.

Supply of Atabrine

(iv) *Time of Action:* After Mess—Preferably the evening meal.

(v) *Technique:* Soldiers line up, and On Call, one proceeds to Lyster Water Bag, with his cup in hand. The enlisted attendant allows water to run into cup to the depth of about ½ inch (a good swallow). Must prevent crowding.

With cup in *left hand*, the Soldier proceeds to Atabrine Tablet (interval from next Soldier not less than 3 feet)—to avoid efforts at non-compliance.

The appropriate dose of Atabrine is delivered into the outstretched *right hand* (by other Enlisted Attendant). Under no condition is Soldier permitted to "help himself" to the Atabrine Tablets. NOW, without closing his right hand, the Soldier facing the supervising Officer, next tossing the Atabrine into his mouth, drinks the entire contents of the canteen Cup, and then inverts the empty Cup squarely upon the table—all under the supervision of the Officer, from *start to finish*.

The Soldier next proceeds to the "checker" (the NCO), giving Name, Rank and Organization, and waits until name is checked on List, keeping the 3-foot interval from adjacent Soldier to avoid jamming. After his name is checked off List, he then "falls in—at ease" in second formation (in ranks), where men are observed for 5 minutes to detect any unauthorized effort at improper disposal of the Atabrine.

Atabrine discipline must be excellent ! ! !

(vi) *Results:* This supervised administration of Atabrine often has caused a *complete cessation* of recurrent attacks of malaria in large bodies of Men (in all situations) who previously were subjected to episodes of this disease. This arrangement may be modified to *meet combat conditions up front*.

(3) *Selection of camp and bivouac sites* will be made so as to avoid if possible:

(a) Proximity to native villages of camps. (Curfew—native laborers will not be permitted in camp or bivouac area between sunset and sunrise.)

(b) Areas known to have a heavy population of malaria carrying mosquitoes,—disapproved by the Malariologist.

(4) *Individual protective measures* will be carried out as follows:

(a) Wearing of shorts and shirts without sleeves is prohibited. All troops will wear shirt sleeves rolled down from sunset to sunrise. Leggings will be worn to protect ankles and legs from mosquito bites and from injuries leading to tropical sores.

(b) All personnel will be required to sleep under mosquito nets. Unit commanders will instruct troops in using sleeping nets; and by frequent inspections at night will see that nets are efficiently used.

(c) Mosquito headnets and gloves will be worn while on guard duty or other night work whenever possible. Officers and men who, because of their work are unable to wear gloves and headnets, will cover all exposed skin surfaces with repellent—repeat every few hours.

(5) *Anti-mosquito measures*, as follows, will be initiated immediately upon arrival in malarious areas:

(a) Hand killing of engorged mosquitoes will be done daily in each tent and hut within the area.

(b) Each tent, hut, or sleeping place will be sprayed daily with insecticide to kill the infected mosquitoes.

(c) Breeding places for mosquito larvae within half a mile radius of the camp will be drained, filled or oiled by unit anti-malaria detail. Especial attention will be directed to standing water in man-made excavations, wheel ruts, coconut shells, can, and other containers. It is the commanding officer's responsibility to see that the program for destruction of breeding places is efficiently carried out.

(d) Spraying by airplane with DDT of entire area is recommended for control of all disease bearing insects.

7. DENGUE.—

This fever has caused considerable suffering and non-effectiveness among military personnel. Its prevention lies entirely in eliminating mosquito breeding and avoiding their bites as discussed under Malaria.

8. SCRUB TYPHUS.—

Incidence low but important because of a death rate of approximately 5%. Ordinary typhus vaccine offers no protection. Use of insect repellents, clearing away vegetation and avoiding, when possible, areas of tropical growth are only known measures for avoiding infection. Combat troops and others should be issued and compelled to wear clothing impregnated with DDT.

9. DYSENTERY.—

Dysentery is usually prevalent among natives who often act as carriers. They should not be employed around army messes. Native food and water are dangerous. The water should be purified and all food cooked thoroughly before eating.

Strict waste disposal sanitation should be enforced. All human excreta should be covered to prevent flies gaining access to it. Teach men to wash hands before eating, using water from canteen, if necessary. Where water cannot be heated for mess kit sterilization, requisition "Compound, Germicidal Rinse." One unit is sufficient for 200 mess kits. It is packed 96 units to a case. One case lasts 200 men one month. There is no automatic supply—it must be requisitioned. In forward areas, instruct men to sterilize their spoons with chlorinated water or to wash hands if they are eating "C" rations with fingers. Like all other preventive measures, sanitation discipline must be continuous to be effective. Any relaxation is sure to be followed by an outbreak of disease.

10. VENEREAL DISEASES.—

Very prevalent among the natives, whose moral standard may be considered none too high. Barter of cigarettes, tobacco, candy, and chocolate bar or other food, a cake of soap, or even quinine tablets (very much in demand by natives) may provide the soldier with sexual contact. Keep men away from native villages, and have well marked prophylactic stations available and their location known to the command. Instruction in VD prevention, and good *DISCIPLINE* of troops will show results here.

11. INSECTS AND SNAKES.—

a. *Ticks, Leeches, and Chiggers*, should be sought for once or more daily, and ticks and leeches carefully removed. A wet cigarette butt or some grease will loosen them, making removal easy and complete. Tweezers may be used, then touch the wound with tincture of iodine to disinfect it.

b. *Chiggers* may produce extensive skin lesions, especially if site of bites are scratched. Powdered sulphur or "DDT" in sox and around waist band may lessen the number of bites. Phenol ointment (or lotion) or iodine may be used. Avoid sitting directly on ground, dead stumps, or logs. Insect repellent sprayed on the clothing of lower legs, arms and around neck affords some protection against both ticks and chiggers, also wearing of impregnated clothing.

c. *Sand Flies* are a nuisance at night, irritating and persistent. They are so small they pass through ordinary screens, being attracted by lights at night. Free use of insect repellent and sleeping under very fine mesh mosquito bar at night is good procedure. DDT on screens is effective.

d. *Snakes*. Snakes thrive in the tropics, in Central and South America, in Australia and East Indies. The Cobra is found in Malaya, India and the Philippines. Troops should be taught to avoid being bitten and should be cautioned against walking barefooted, or placing hands on ledges or logs where they cannot see what is there. Most bites are on hands and forearms, feet, ankles and the lower part of the legs. The actual number of persons bitten is relatively small—*deaths RARE.*

Company aid men should be well qualified to give emergency treatment for snake bite, by applying some form of tourniquet (shoe lace), incising the wound, *massaging and sucking same at once.* Kill snake for identification and send for the medical officer without delay. *KEEP PATIENT QUIET—AT REST.*

12. NATIVE VILLAGES.—

Assume every tropical native village to be infected with: Venereal Diseases; Typhoid and Dysentery; Smallpox; Malarial Fever; Intestinal Parasites (all types); and in the Southwest Pacific, possibly Plague, Cholera and Typhus Fever. During campaign, villages and native huts should be shunned by troops, and patrols should see that troops do not enter for pleasure purposes. *OFF LIMITS!* Camping in the immediate vicinity of native villages is very undesirable. One mile away from the camp (bivouac) is good SOP.

13. FIELD SERVICE IN THE TROPICS.—

Troops should be relieved every three or four months for rest and recuperation if the tactical situation permits, otherwise a large noneffective rate due to illness will develop. Send them to a Rest Camp up in the hills or at a clean beach to get good food, much-needed sleep, rest, recreation, recuperation and rehabilitation.

14. EVACUATION AND HOSPITALIZATION.—

The following general plan for evacuation and hospitalization was successful employed by an American Division during active combat operations under jungle conditions. Its success is attributed to fitting the means at hand to the existing problem. Army litter bearers, native porters, native canoes, small boats, landing barges, "jeep" ambulances and air transport were employed in echelons of evacuation. Pack animals—if available—would have been helpful.

Medical service for each of three regimental task forces (CT's) consisted of regimental medical detachment, a collecting company plus three portable surgical hospitals (4 Officers and 33 Enlisted Men each). The collecting company organized into three similar platoons—each containing a station section, a litter bearer section and an ambulance section—each infantry battalion having one of these platoons attached, plus a supporting portable surgical hospital for definite surgery.

1st Echelon of Evacuation was performed by medical sections of infantry battalions with their Aid Stations established as far forward as possible—within two or three hundred yards—concealed and defiladed—on dry ground.

2d Echelon of Evacuation was carried out by the attached collecting platoon, its collecting station established beyond mortar range—some 800 to 1,500 yards back in thick jungle—concealed and camouflaged, near a trail. All sick and wounded being evacuated walked to the collecting station or were transported by litter bearers. Immediate surgery cases were promptly taken on litters to the portable surgical hospital nearby where many operations were performed daily. Those less seriously wounded and the sick who should not be retained, were sent to the clearing station, using "jeeps" if practicable. Patients who might be returned to duty in two or three days remained at the collecting station for treatment. Sorting was thus accomplished carefully at the collecting station. Native bearers were very helpful.

The 3d Echelon of Evacuation began at the clearing station, usually located two or three miles further to the rear, where much surgery was performed. After a proper rest period of several days patients were taken by "jeep" ambulances over the trail to the Field Hospital (acting evacuation hospital) which had been established near a landing strip. Casualties requiring further hospitalization and treatment were transported by cargo plane (C-47's), one hundred or more miles away, to station and evacuation hospitals (under canvas) located in Advance or Base Sections on the Lines of Communication.

15. SUMMARY.—

The following precautions have been recommended by Surgeons for troops fighting under jungle conditions in the Southwest Pacific area:

   a. *Prevention of Malarial Fevers.*

      (1) Sleep under Mosquito Bar—tucked in well—KILL ANY TRAPPED MOSQUITOES.

      (2) Use Headnet and gauntlets when out at night. Use Repellents.

      (3) TAKE ATABRINE AS DIRECTED—Helps PREVENT malarial fevers.

      (4) Wear Long Trousers and Shirt Sleeves to reduce number of insect bites. Wear impregnated clothing in highly malarious areas.

      (5) Each Company and Battery Anti-Malaria Squad will:

         (a) Seek and destroy local mosquito breeding areas;

         (b) Fumigate dug-outs daily;

(c) Be constantly alert for violation of above requirements.

  b. *High Standards of Hygiene and Sanitation.*

    (1) Observe strict water discipline.

    (2) Use Salt tablets as directed.

    (3) Avoid Chilling by:

      (a) Sleeping Dry;

      (b) Not sleeping on wet ground;

      (c) Covering abdomen and chest at night.

    (4) Keep SKIN clean by:

      (a) Bathing daily—using soap;

      (b) Disinfecting cuts and using powder on sore spots;

      (c) Changing sox often.

    (5) Wash clothing at least twice a week, and dry it out.

    (6) Keep your immediate area properly sanitated.

  c. *What To Do If Wounded.*

    (1) Take SULFA tablets as directed.

    (2) Dust wound with SULFA powder and apply dressing.

    (3) Move off trail—away from Jap Sniper. Call for help.

    (4) DON'T LOSE OR FORGET YOUR JUNGLE MEDICAL KIT.

16. CONCLUSION.—

Well disciplined troops, experienced with jungle training will not find service under jungle conditions prejudicial to good health, but they must be WELL DISCIPLINED in every sense of the word.

STUDY AND KNOW THE JUNGLE, AND THUS MAKE IT YOUR ALLY!!!

Malaria: A Pamphlet for Officers

1. MALARIA AND THE SOLDIER

1. Introduction

(*a*) Malaria can ruin your health permanently; it can destroy the fighting efficiency of an army.

(*b*) Yet it is a disease which can be avoided if certain precautions are taken.

(*c*) Malaria is sure to exist in greater or lesser degree in the tropical countries in which you are likely to serve. In some places near the Equator it occurs throughout the year, in others it is limited to a season, generally June to November.

(*d*) Campaigns should be arranged, if possible, to coincide with the non-malarial season where one exists. Otherwise, malaria becomes a more important factor in planning and executing every operation.

(*e*) In the tropics this disease can kill or injure you just as surely as can a bullet, and the ability to fight it successfully demands as high a degree of training and discipline as does the battle against the human enemy.

(*f*) In some ways malaria is more formidable than the human enemy. Its sphere of activity may cover the whole theatre of operations. It is always threatening you and you can never afford to relax your watch.

(*g*) A battle, even a campaign, can be lost without a bullet being fired. History records many instances.

(*h*) But just as a sand bag, a tank, or a pill box can afford you protection from bullets, so also can protection be given you against this disease if you will only take advantage of it.

(*i*) In their duty of looking after the welfare and health of their men, all officers must appreciate the important part that anti-malarial measures play. The responsibility is theirs and not the medical officer's; he is only the expert adviser.

(*j*) Measures of attack and defence cannot be left to the medical officer. To be effective every man from the commander to the private soldier must play his party. There must be no shirkers. The same strict discipline is demanded as is required in battle.

2. How is malaria contracted?

(*a*) The mosquito is the culprit.

(*b*) Not all mosquitoes carry malaria. The dangerous one is the ANOPHELINE, and only certain anophelines, and only those which are infected, can transmit the disease. Since, however, it is impossible for the ordinary soldier to distinguish friend from foe, all mosquitoes must be treated as enemies.

(*c*) The mosquito becomes infected by biting a person suffering from malaria or having the germs in his blood.

(*d*) After the mosquito has had its blood meal it takes 10 days before it can infect a healthy individual. It does this in the process of biting.

(*e*) You will see that for malaria to spread three things are required:—

    i. An infected person.

    ii. An infective mosquito.

    iii. A healthy man—possibly yourself.

3. How can it be prevented?

(*a*) If we could remove the germs from all individuals in the tropics, mosquitoes could not become infected and there would be no malaria.

(*b*) If we could destroy all anopheline mosquitoes, there would be no agent to transmit the disease and there would be no malaria.

(*c*) Theoretically both these measures should be possible, in practice neither is.

(*d*) We can, however, do a great deal towards this end, but have to admit that in many instances the task is beyond our power.

(*e*) If it were possible to prevent the mosquito from biting the healthy person, there would eventually be no malaria.

(*f*) You are given the means of protection, and if you conscientiously obey instructions the changes of your getting the disease will be greatly lessened. Under active service conditions in the field, personal protection is the most important of all methods of malaria prevention. Failure to observe personal protective measures is tantamount to self-inflicted injury and demands strong disciplinary action.

(*g*) There are circumstances of course, in which full protection cannot be provided and heavier casualties from malaria must be expected. In battle, for instance, a soldier is more concerned with dodging bullets than mosquitoes and cannot be expected to take the necessary precautions; nor can he carry with him all his anti-mosquito equipment.

(*h*) Let us now study the three links in the chain of infection and see how we can break or, at least, weaken them.

(*i*) If a soldier in your unit is suffering from malaria, he can be rendered harmless if he is kept under a mosquito net; the mosquitoes cannot get at him, and so fail to become infective.

(*j*) But the most common source of malaria is the local inhabitant. He generally goes about only half clad and therefore mosquitoes have glorious opportunities to feed on him; not does he use a mosquito net at night.

(*k*) Keep clear of his dwelling places when you can.

4. Measures to control mosquitoes breeding

(*a*) To destroy the mosquito by preventing its breeding is the main object of all big anti-malaria schemes.

(*b*) One example is all that is necessary. Singapore was a highly malarious town; it was, too, a most important naval base. Before the extension of the post could be undertaken, malaria had to be abolished. This work involved an immense amount of engineering work, mainly irrigation and drainage, and a vast expenditure of money. But it was worth it. Singapore, from being a malarious swamp, became a healthy place and a flourishing port.

(*c*) You will have surmised already that water is in some way associated with malaria.

(*d*) This had been known from the earliest times. It was thought that it was the bad air from swamps that caused the disease; and that is why the disease is called Malaria—"Malus" bad, and "Aër" air.

(*e*) But what our forefathers did not know was that the swamp was unhealthy because it was the breeding place of mosquitoes.

(*f*) Like many other winged insects the mosquito lays its eggs in water, and there the developing insect passes through all its stages from egg to flier.

(*g*) You have perhaps seen little "wigglers" in the water butt at your home. These were probably the larvae of mosquitoes which had hatched out from eggs.

(*h*) Now you can see the importance of draining the land of swamps and all collections of casual water. The more you dry up the land, the fewer places are there for the mosquito to breed.

(*i*) Mosquitoes in the main prefer stagnant fresh water, but some species will breed in saltish water in lagoons and mangrove swamps near the sea, and others prefer the running water at the edge of streams.

(*j*) Even the smallest collections of water in rain gutters and in holes in trees, in fact anything that will hold a few ounces of water, will breed thousands of mosquitoes.

(*k*) It takes about 10 days under the best conditions for the larvae on hatching out to develop into full-grown mosquitoes.

(*l*) Therefore, if you can empty all containers once a week by pouring the contents on to the ground you will do a lot to keep down the mosquito population.

(*m*) But the most effective method is not to permit any tins, etc., which can collect water to be left lying about.

(*n*) The malaria season generally follows the rains. The reason is that every little hole and hollow fills with water and the breeding of mosquitoes is increased manifold.

(*o*) But it is impossible to drain every swamp and lake, and rivers will continue to flow. Moreover, in war, big engineering schemes cannot be undertaken.

(*p*) We have therefore to resort to some means of killing the larvae in the water and we have two very effective methods:

  i. Spraying "Malariol," an oil substance.
  ii. Depositing Paris Green on the surface of the water.

(*q*) The larvae have to come to the surface of the water every now and then, to breathe; if we coat the surface with a thin film of oil, they are suffocated and die. Their death is accelerated by the poisonous action of the oil which is used. This is the purpose of "Malariol."

(*r*) Paris Green contains arsenic. It is blown over the surface of the water, mixed with a light dust. The larvae of the anopheline mosquito feed on the surface, and as the Paris Green floats, the larvae swallow the fine particles and are quickly killed.

(*s*) Anti-mosquito squads are equipped with sprayers and blowers, and a tremendous reduction in the numbers of mosquitoes can be effected by a weekly treatment of all collections of water which cannot be drained.

(*t*) Mosquitoes do not normally fly a long way. In fact, if they can obtain water in which to breed and blood on which to feed close to their resting place, they will fly no farther than is necessary.

(*u*) If an area of half a mile round a camp is either cleared of water, or the water is treated as described, mosquitoes will not bother you much.

(*v*) Of course large clouds of mosquitoes may at times be borne several miles on the wind. In selecting a camp you should choose a site up wind from possible breeding places.

5. Measures against adult mosquitoes

(*a*) We have seen what we can do to reduce the numbers of mosquitoes by attacking their breeding places. How can you destroy the adult mosquito that invades your sleeping quarters, be it a room in a building, a hut, or a tent?

(*b*) The mosquito is a "night bird." It rests during the day in some dark spot, but when the sun is setting (and it sets rapidly in the tropics) it leaves its retreat and takes to the wing, with one or two objects in view, either to lay its eggs or to feed.

(*c*) It is during the night and at evening and sunrise in particular that the mosquito is dangerous.

(*d*) Strange as it may seem, it is only the female that "desires your blood." The male is a perfectly harmless creature, quite satisfied by feeding on the juices of plants.

(*e*) But you cannot easily distinguish the male from the female so the innocent must suffer with the guilty.

(*f*) We have said that the mosquito requires a dark place in which to rest during the day. Do not provide her with one unless it is a trap. You can learn how to make these from the malaria officer.

(*g*) Boots, boxes, cupboards, hanging clothing are favourite hiding places. By a little ingenuity you can disappoint her.

(*h*) If driven outside she will content herself with the best shade provided, such as long grass, bushes, in fact any place that will provide her with both shade and shelter.

(*i*) Cut down the grass and bush around your camp and you will again thwart her.

(*j*) Driven out into the open the strong tropical sun will eventually kill her.

(*k*) By this means you can reduce the numbers of mosquitoes that will share your quarters, but some will still find their way in. These can be killed by using an anti-mosquito spray or by swatting with a fly-swatter. Each unit is provided with a supply of these.

(*l*) The best time to do "the killing" is after dusk or, better still, just after dawn.

(*m*) To be effective, spraying must be carried out regularly and one man should be detailed to do the work. Every corner and nook and cranny of the room should be sprayed.

(*n*) Another very important area to be sprayed will be the houses of the adjacent village, if one exists, and any outbuildings, stables, garages, etc., in barracks, but this will be the duty of the anti-malarial squad working under the malaria officer.

(*o*) Spraying is probably the most important of all general anti-malaria measures under active service conditions. Apparatus has recently been devised which can release the solution into the room as a very fine mist or fog, killing all mosquitoes, and remaining overnight to catch any mosquitoes which enter later.

6. Personal protection against mosquitoes

(*a*) How can you protect yourself?

(*b*) You may be fortunate in being provided with a mosquito-proofed quarter, that is, one in which all windows, doors, and ventilation openings are screened with fine wire gauze. (Do not mistake fly-proofing, which is fairly common in the tropics, for mosquito-proofing, which is rare.) It should not be necessary for you to take other precautions while indoors, but it is wise to have a search round each day for mosquitoes, and use the sprayer if they are found. Doors in a mosquito-proofed building must never, of course, be propped open.

(*c*) If you are not so fortunate, then you must use your mosquito net. You must learn to use it properly and to take care of it.

(*d*) Before sunset you should tuck the bottom well in under your mattress or blankets, and be careful when turning in at night not to allow any mosquitoes in with you.

(*e*) The net does not stand hard treatment. Be kind to it.

(*f*) Inspect it carefully from time to time, and if any holes or tears are present sew them up at once.

(*g*) Officers should hold regular unit net inspections to see that all nets are kept in good repair, and should pay surprise visits after sundown to see that nets are down and properly tucked in.

(*h*) The mosquito net has been dealt with first as it is your most important means of protection, but few of you will have retired to bed at dusk when the mosquitoes come out.

(*i*) How then are you going to guard yourself against the attack of mosquitoes?

(*j*) There are two main ways :—

i. By keeping your body as completely clothed as possible.

ii. By using on the exposed parts, face and hands, some substance repellent to the mosquito.

(*k*) At sundown and after you must wear trousers and shirts buttoned at the wrists. Shorts and sleeveless shirts should be strictly forbidden. Remember that mosquitoes can bite through socks; boots, and if possible, puttees should be worn, or two pairs of socks.

(*l*) Every soldier is given a small tin container. See that it is filled with anti-mosquito cream.

(*m*) This cream will keep mosquitoes off for only two hours at the most. Its effects will wear off more quickly when you are working and sweating.

(*n*) It is a sticky substance and not too pleasant when smeared on your face, but until something better is discovered you will have to put up with it. You must use anti-mosquito cream on all occasions when mosquitoes are prevalent.

(*o*) It should be applied thoroughly and liberally to the hands and exposed skin of the head and neck. The forehead and ears require special attention.

7. Protection during active operations

(*a*) Some of the measures described may be suitable only when you are living under static conditions. During active operations the risk of exposure will be much greater and the means of protection correspondingly less.

Very similar measures can be taken, though not with the same degree of effectiveness.

(*b*) i. Long trousers and long sleeved shirts should be worn.

ii. For men who are on picket or sentry duty, special veils and gauntlets are provided.

iii. Repellent cream should be used more frequently and more lavishly.

iv. A mosquito net which can be carried by you and erected when required has been devised. It has pouches at the bottom which can be filled with sand, earth, or stones. These have the effect of keeping it close to the ground. It is called a bush net.

v. Bivouac tents and shelters mosquito proofed with netting are also supplied. The bivouac net used as a lining to tents and shelters can also be erected separately. It accommodates two persons.

(c) The methods described have as their purpose the prevention of the mosquito biting you and giving you malaria.

(d) Should you be bitten there is a second line of defence against the disease. This is what is known as the "suppressive treatment" of malaria. Quinine and mepacrine are the drugs used.

(e) These drugs do not always prevent your being infected; the germs may enter and remain in your body, but an "attack of malaria" may be warded off. Quinine or mepacrine when used in the recommended dose only keeps the germs suppressed or under control.

(f) You can see how vital this measure is when other means of prevention are absent or only partial. An army which, without this aid, would disintegrate though malaria, can be kept in the field more or less fit for an indefinite period. Cases which do occur in spite of precautions will only be a fraction of the numbers which would have gone sick without this type of protection.

(g) You must realize, however, that if the drugs are not taken regularly when your medical officer advises, their effects will be partial only.

(h) The dose varies with the degree of prevalence of malaria in the area in question. An area in which malaria is very common is known as a hyperendemic area, and large doses of suppressive drugs are necessary. In areas in which it is not so prevalent (areas of moderate or low "endemicity") smaller doses are sufficient. Enquiry should be made beforehand, and the appropriate system of dosage adopted throughout the force.

(i) i. In a hyperendemic area, suppressive quinine should be given in doses of 10 grains (two tablets) every evening at sundown. The men should be paraded under an officer who should witness that every man of his platoon or company takes his dose. Nobody should be excused or overlooked. The drug is more effective in solution but bottles of medicine are hardly practicable in the field. If taken in tablet form they should be broken in two and followed by a draught of water.

ii. Where malaria is present, but not hyperendemic, suppressive quinine is given in doses of 5 grains (one tablet) every evening. Apart from the reduction in dose, the instructions are the same as for hyperendemic areas.

(j) Quinine should be begun on the day of arrival in a malarious country, where full mosquito protection cannot be ensured, and should be continued throughout the whole period of residence, and for a month after leaving.

(*k*) It is more than likely that when the quinine is dropped a number of men will go sick with fever. This result must be expected. From a military point of view it does not matter—the battle is over and won. You have done your part in keeping fit while it was raging. Many will escape the disease altogether, and any who do go sick after the operation is over can go to hospital and be cured.

(*l*) *Suppressive mepacrine* is likely to be the drug which you will be given in future. Since Java fell into the hands of the Japs, quinine supplies from this island (where it was mainly grown) have had to be conserved for the treatment of actual cases of malaria.

(*m*) Mepacrine, unlike quinine, must be commenced a week before entering the malarious area of operations. It must be continued throughout, and for a month after leaving the danger area.

(*n*) i. In a hyperendemic area, the dose of suppressive mepacrine is one tablet (0.1 gramme) every day of the week except Sunday. The men should be paraded in the same way as for quinine.

ii. Where malaria is less prevalent, suppressive mepacrine is taken on two days in each week only, with an interval of two days between each dose. The dose is two tablets (0.1 gramme each) on each of these days, the first taken with water after breakfast, the second in the same manner after dinner.

(*o*) Don't be surprised if your skin becomes slightly yellow. It is only a dye and of no significance.

(*p*) If, while you are on suppressive quinine or mepacrine, you feel that in spite of your precautions you are developing malaria, it is quite safe to take treble the dose suggested above for hyperendemic areas, for three or four days. That is, you may increase the dose to two tablets of quinine or one of mepacrine three times daily. If possible, consult the medical officer before increasing the dose, and return to the prescribed routine of suppressive treatment after three or four days.

8. Symptoms of malaria

(*a*) But what is this disease we have been talking about, and what are the symptoms for us to recognize when it occurs?

(*b*) Malaria is caused by a parasite or germ which is injected into the blood by the anopheline mosquito.

(*c*) There are three different kinds of malaria parasites, but the two important ones are those responsible for the malignant and benign types of fever.

(*d*) As the names imply, the malignant type is the more severe and is by far the most dangerous of the three. The benign or mild type can give you some unpleasant moments, and will reduce your fitness temporarily, but you need not be afraid of it.

(*e*) The typical attack of malaria lasts a week to ten days, that is if you are under proper treatment, and you will experience three distinct stages or phases during your illness.

(*f*) There is first the *shivering stage*. Although you find the greatest difficulty in keeping warm, your temperature is high, you have a severe headache, and feel sick. The attack of shivering comes on suddenly.

(*g*) Then next comes the *sweating stage* when you feel burning hot and are drenched in sweat, having to change your shirt and underclothes, or pyjamas and sheets frequently. You will probably feel somewhat better during this stage than during the first.

(*h*) Then there is the *stage of collapse*. You are not really collapsed in the true sense of the word. In fact you feel much relieved, your temperature has dropped, your headache will probably have gone, and the sweating has ceased. You feel weak as if you have been "through it," as indeed you have. You will probably turn over on your side and sleep this stage out.

(*i*) It is hoped that you will be under medical care shortly after the attack of malaria starts, to ensure that you can be properly treated and looked after.

(*j*) If you feel headachey and unwell, report sick. It is no use fighting against malaria. Get proper treatment, otherwise you will have relapses and they may occur at very awkward times when hospital treatment may be far off.

(*k*) With the malignant type of malaria the symptoms may be very varied and will certainly be more severe. Sometimes the patient becomes unconscious, or may have severe vomiting or diarrhoea or chest symptoms, which obscure the true nature of his illness. At any rate, he feels very ill and the hospital is the only place for him, and the sooner he is there under treatment the sooner will he be well again.

(*l*) If you feel sick and off-colour in the topics always suspect malaria as being the cause, and "go sick."

(*m*) If you follow the advice given in these notes and drill yourself to carry out the measures laid down with scrupulous attention from the first day of your arrival, a great many of you will avoid the disease, and, from the point of view of malaria, will come home as fit as, if not fitter than, when you went out.

(*n*) Why ruin your health when it can be avoided?

EQUIPMENT, NAVIGATION AND CAMOUFLAGE

British and Indian soldiers wore standard 'khaki drill' uniform in 1941–42, from the Indian word *khak* meaning dust and the uniform was made from a 'drilled' cotton fabric. However the colour and the use of shorts were entirely unsuitable for the jungle. This was replaced by jungle-green uniforms in 1943, which comprised Aertex battle dress shirt, trousers and bush jacket that helped camouflage and reduced exposure to insect bites in the jungle. The high humidity of the jungle tended to rot fabric and leather quickly: standard army issue boots disintegrated in about ten days. American jungle boots were eventually adopted across the two theatres.

Weapons were also adapted for the jungle. The 25-pdr gun used by all British and Commonwealth Armies was too heavy and wide to be towed by a jeep along jungle tracks as well as be carried by air. The 129th Field Regiment experimented with guns by fitting a jeep axle and wheels, which improved both movement in the jungle and air portability. The adapted gun became known as the 'jury axle' 25-pdr. Artillery support was essential in the jungle but was not always possible due to the dense undergrowth of the jungle. Then support was provided by 3in. and 2in. mortars. These were modified for jungle use with the base plate of the 3in. mortar strengthened and a new sight installed that increased the range to 2,750 yards. The Mark 5 version of the 3in. mortar was a specially designed lighter version for use in the jungles of South East Asia but only 5,000 were produced before the end of the war. Similarly, the 2in. mortar was fixed with a 'bowed' plate that reduced its weight without affecting its accuracy and range.

Military Training Pamphlet No. 9 (India)
The Jungle Book

XIII. ADMINISTRATION.

11. Ammunition.—On occasions, additional ammunition will have to be carried in the same manner as supplies. It has been found that, in emergency, the following can be carried for limited periods, in addition to reserve rations and the personal equipment of the individual soldier:—

.303	100 rounds per rifleman
.303	8 magazines per Bren.
.45	200 rounds per sub-machine gun.
2" Mortar	12 rounds per mortar.
3" Mortar	24 bombs per platoon.
Grenades	Average two per man throughout unit.

A reserve of fuses for Mortar bombs must be carried, since these cannot be dropped from the air.

Ammunition, whether carried in pouches, bandoliers or magazines must be cleaned regularly to prevent deterioration in the jungle. Each round of ammunition dropped from the air must be examined to eliminate damaged or bulged rounds. If this has not been done by ordnance personnel, battalions must conduct their own inspections.

Field Manual 72-20
Jungle Warfare

Section III. WEAPONS, CLOTHING, AND EQUIPMENT

Weapons

a. Weapons must often be reduced to those which, with the required amount of ammunition, can be carried by the troops themselves or on the limited transport capable of moving with the troops. This frequently reduces the number of supporting weapons, requiring that tactical plans be based mainly on the use of weapons which can be carried by hand and which do not use too much nor too heavy ammunition. Decisions concerning the amounts and kinds of ammunition and weapons to be carried are command decisions which must be made by the local commander after careful consideration of the difficulties of transport and the types of weapons needed to accomplish his mission. Hand and rifle grenades and mortars, although heavy and difficult to transport, are highly effective jungle weapons; small-caliber weapons and ammunition, though less difficult to transport, are inadequate by themselves for the accomplishment of any large-scale mission.

b. Suitable weapons for use in jungle warfare, where observation and fields of fire are very limited, are short-range arms easily supplied with ammunition and readily transported over difficult terrain. The weapons which best meet the above conditions are the rifle and bayonet, automatic rifle, carbine, pistol, submachine gun, hand and rifle grenades, machete, and trench knife. The submachine gun and pistol have the advantage of using the same type of lightweight ammunition. The bayonet should be sufficiently short to reduce danger of its becoming entangled in vines and foliage. Hand grenades are the most important defensive weapons for night attacks and are invaluable in attacking dug-in positions; they may also be used in booby traps. Each rifleman should carry five or six hand grenades. The machete, a tool indispensable to the jungle soldier, is also an excellent weapon for close combat.

c. Light and heavy machine guns and 60-mm and 81-mm mortars are less maneuverable, less suited to instant use, and require ammunition more difficult to transport; however, they are very valuable and can be transported by pack, small carts, or on the backs of men. Lightweight, 60-mm and 81-mm mortars, specially designed for jungle use, are more easily transported, and their effectiveness in jungle warfare is equal to that of the heavier models.

Rocket launchers, firing either high explosive or white phosphorous rockets, are desirable for use against caves and well constructed defensive positions; flame throwers are also effective against such positions.

d. While light, mobile units are an essential in jungle warfare, their armament may be insufficient for the attack of strongly organized positions. Other troops, with heavier weapons, must be moved up rapidly to reinforce advanced units once such a position is uncovered. It must be borne in mind that jungle regions often adjoin savannas or other open areas, in which jungle growth is relatively sparse, as well as villages and towns from which artillery and other supporting ground weapons can be effectively employed. The prompt preparation of trails and roads for rapid movement of artillery is one of the primary missions of engineers. In preparing for operations in jungle regions, a careful preliminary study of terrain conditions in the probable area of operations will aid the commander materially in determining the composition and armament for the forces involved.

Clothing and Equipment

a. Each item of clothing and equipment must be considered in terms of its necessity, and serviceability in jungle environment. Lightness of weight is essential because of the difficulties of transport. Serviceability is essential, because of the problems of resupply. Every effort should be made to reduce to the minimum the amount of equipment to be used, but care should be exercised that no essential items are omitted. During training, men should be required to use only items of clothing and equipment which will be taken into combat areas; not only will this teach them to live with a minimum of essentials, but also it may indicate the nonessentiality of some things originally thought to be necessary. Clothing worn during training should be of the same color and pattern as that to be worn in combat. To change will create additional difficulty in identification of friendly troops at a time when reduced visibility necessarily creates an identification problem.

b. Tight-fitting clothing is unsatisfactory, since such clothing is hot and restricts movement. Articles of clothing and equipment made of wool, leather, or felt have proven unsatisfactory for jungle use because of their heat-retaining qualities, absorption of moisture, and susceptibility to mold and fungus rot. Such articles should be replaced whenever possible by cotton, rubber, and canvas items. As an article of outer clothing, the combat suit, two-piece, dark green, herringbone twill, has been found highly satisfactory. Rubber-soled canvas boots are desirable for stealthy movement through the jungle, but are hard on the feet if worn for long periods. The issue field shoe, with composition sole, is satisfactory for general use. In some rocky areas, hobnails in the soles of the shoes are desirable. The helmet liner, M1, has been found to be much more satisfactory than the fatigue hat for jungle wear. In combat, the steel helmet may be easily camouflaged by the use of leaves and twigs held in place by a rubber band, or by the helmet net. A mosquito-proof head net and gloves are an inseparable part of each individual's equipment. A raincoat or a lightweight combination poncho and shelter half is indispensable.

Care of Weapons, Clothing, and Equipment

a. Weapons, clothing, and equipment receive hard usage in the jungle. Men must be trained to protect all articles and to clean, dry, or repair them whenever practicable. Our weapons and equipment are the best and will not become unserviceable unless neglected, but the damp heat of jungle areas requires that special care be given to all weapons and other nonrustproof equipment in daily or frequent use. The humidity, the mud, and the frequent shortage of oil and other materials necessary for cleaning weapons combine to make weapon maintenance in the jungle particularly difficult. All weapons and equipment must receive constant preventive maintenance. The potential battle efficiency of a combat unit undergoing training can be determined almost precisely by the condition in which it maintains weapons and equipment. Equally, this reflects the military leadership qualities of its officers and noncommissioned officers.

b. One of the most important duties of subordinate leaders is to carry out frequent personal inspections to determine the state of maintenance of weapons, ammunition, magazines, spare parts, and accessories. Time and circumstances will rarely permit a thorough inspection of all weapons in a platoon at one time. Under such circumstances, frequent random inspections or spot checks will be made.

c. (1) All personnel (including officers) of a unit operating in the jungle should carry individual small cans of preservative lubricating oil. Extra oil must be carried by members of machine-gun squads.

(2) In hot, humid climates, light or special preservative lubricating oil should be used on weapons; in saltwater atmospheres, medium preservative lubricating oil should be used.

(3) Three or four cleaning rods must be carried in each rifle squad. Patches should be carried by each individual.

(4) Weapons must be disassembled, inspected, and cleaned daily; in rainy weather, it may be necessary to do this 2 or 3 times a day. By laying rifles on crotched sticks several inches off the ground at night, and placing banana leaves over them, they can be kept dry.

(5) Breech mechanisms can be protected by tying an oil-soaked cloth around them. This should be attached in such a manner that the cloth can be easily removed by means of a quick pull on one end.

(6) Wooden parts of weapons should be inspected to see that swelling caused by moisture does not cause binding of the working parts. (If swelling has occurred, shave off *only enough* wood to relieve the binding.) A light coat of raw linseed oil applied at intervals and well rubbed in with the heel of the hand will help to keep out moisture. Allow oil to soak in for a few hours and then wipe and polish the wood with a dry, clean rag. Care should be taken to see that linseed oil does not get into the mechanism or on metal parts, as it will gum up when dry. The stock and hand guard should be dismounted when this oil is applied.

(7) Accessories, spare parts, and magazines will rust and deteriorate rapidly if not cared for diligently.

(8) Optical equipment such as mortar sights, compasses, and field glasses should receive special care. Field glasses and compasses, when not in use, should be protected from moisture.

(9) All machetes must be sharpened and oiled before going into a jungle operation. If one man in the squad carries a small commercial stone, it will be found helpful for sharpening machete blades which soon get badly dulled and nicked.

(10) Tropical insects, especially termites and ants, will often damage or destroy fabrics or wood in a few hours. Therefore, whenever practicable, clothing and equipment should be *hung off the ground*, away from most of the destructive insects. Troops leaders must check each night to see that their men hang their clothing, packs, shoes, etc., from bushes, ropes, or other available supports.

(11) Exposing clothing and equipment to sunlight to dry them and kill germs is desirable. However, unnecessary exposure of fabrics to intense tropical sunlight weakens them and bleaches even the best of dyes. Camouflaged uniforms will fade more, quickly if they are left for hours in the sunlight.

Figure 2. Poncho used as raincoat.

Figure 3. Ponchos used as sleeping bag.

Figure 4. Ponchos used as sun shelters.

d. A tendency exists to turn in dirty clothes and to draw new whenever possible, rather than to launder the dirty clothes. When the situation is an active one, this is to be expected, as no time exists for washing clothes. When the situation is stabilized, and time, soap, and water are available, dirty clothes should be boiled and washed. Enforcement of these provisions is a function of command.

e. Immediate disciplinary action must be taken when men waste or lose their equipment through carelessness. Much equipment will be unavoidably lost or damaged incident to training and active operations. Such losses are legitimate, but wastage due to carelessness is a serious military offense.

Section IV. PRACTICAL HINTS FOR JUNGLE LIVING

Sleeping

a. During the dry season, men can sleep comfortably on the ground. They must, however, sleep under mosquito nets.

b. (1) When sleeping in the jungle during the rainy season, a man must be off the ground and under a mosquito net. This is best accomplished by the use of an insect-proof hammock fabricated of light, durable, waterproof material. The hammock should be furnished with a rainproof, adjustable top with attachable insect netting, and should not exceed six pounds in weight complete with netting. In dry weather, a man can sleep on the ground in a sleeping bag improvised from ponchos (see figs. 2 and 3).

(2) Lacking a hammock similar to the one described above, improvised hammocks or jungle beds may be used. Hammocks are made of blankets, oblong pieces of canvas, or shelter halves. A two-man, *off-the-ground* jungle bed may be made as follows: Four forked posts are firmly planted in the ground, the forks one foot above the ground. A frame of 2-inch poles is laid in the forks; across this frame thinner poles are laid. Poles are fastened together with vines or strips of bark. The platform is then covered with light branches and leaves to form a mattress. Care must be exercised that the branches and leaves used for this purpose are free of insects. A blanket is then spread over this mattress to hold everything in place; over all are pitched the shelter tent and mosquito net, or in dry weather, only the mosquito net.

Jungle Navigation

a. For determining direction without compass, map reading in the field, and use of the compass, see FM 21-75 and FM 21-25.

b. Land navigation is one of the most important subjects of special training for jungle operations. Without a good knowledge of this subject, control is impossible. Without control, excellence in other phases of training goes for naught. The ability of all commanders and leaders to maintain control enhances the fighting value of the unit.

Figure 5. Ponchos used as tents.

c. Density of vegetation makes jungle navigation difficult by day or night. Maps are seldom dependable for accurate portrayal of roads and trails which quickly become unrecognizable through erosion and undergrowth when not in constant use. Aerial photographs of jungle terrain seldom show more than the treetops, while limited fields of vision restrict the use of the compass. These difficulties can be overcome, however, by training the individual soldier in jungle navigation in the jungle. This consists of training of the individual's faculties, as well as training in use of the artificial aids given him.

d. If the use of trails is not restricted by tactical considerations, they should be followed in the interest of rapid progress. A study of map trails should be made before starting on the mission. It is usually safe to assume that trails exist between important villages, even though not shown on the map.

e. Navigation through the jungle without dependence on roads and trails requires considerable map-reading ability. It implies skill in following a predetermined route through terrain which offers no landmarks, and knowing constantly one's location with reference to the starting point. To do this successfully one must know the relationship between direction and the distance covered.

f. Successful jungle navigation will be facilitated by:

(1) Movements of short distances at a time, 100 to 300 yards, with frequent checks of map with ground, measuring back azimuths with the compass when practicable. Direction once lost in the jungle is very difficult to regain.

(2) An up-to-date large-scale map or route sketch, preferably 1/25,000 or larger, together with a compass in good working condition.

(3) Navigating personnel. These include a map reader, a compass man, a recorder of detail, and a distance measurer who counts his strides, and computes distance covered by elapsed time. Personnel of this type should be thoroughly trained in advance.

g. Jungle navigators should be trained in the jungle. There is no substitute for this type of training.

h. If a man becomes lost, he should sit down and think calmly. He should ask himself these questions: Were my compass calculations correct? Where did I get off the route? In most cases, careful, calm thought will reveal where he went wrong.

i. The question of the route to be followed and the method of maintaining direction will depend upon the size of the objective to be reached. For example: if it is desired to reach a river known to be located west of the present position, it is only necessary to strike out through the jungle, following the easiest route, but maintaining a general westerly direction. If the traveling is fairly easy and the route followed does not wind too much, the river should eventually be reached. If, however, it is desired to reach a native village which the map shows to be located on this river and due west of the present position, more precise navigation methods must be employed. Two possible routes could be followed to the village; first, a straight line going up and down the mountains and possibly across a swamp or two, or secondly, a course following a circuitous path, but one so controlled as to come out on the river at the village. The first route is the shortest one, but should not be the one chosen unless the country is reasonably flat, the jungle fairly open, and there are no swamps to cross—a series of conditions seldom found for any great distance in jungle terrain. The route actually followed in most cases should be a combination of the two methods; that is, following a straight line where the going is good, but skirting around a swamp or hill. If any route but a straight line is followed, however, it is necessary to keep a plotted record of the directions and distances travelled, in order to reach a final objective as small as a village.

j. In choosing the route, the general rule is that walking is usually best on the ridges and most difficult on the banks of the rivers (except small, fast streams with traversable beds). The jungle is usually more open on the ridges, drainage is good, and the ground is therefore less muddy. In addition, since walking is easiest on the ridges, animals and men have often made trails there. Walking along the river bank is likely to be difficult because of dense, second-growth jungle, mud, swamps, and side streams. The general rule therefore is to walk on the top of the ridges if they run in the right direction. If they do not, walk in the river valleys, but well back from the river's edge. If it is necessary to travel in the valley of a small stream, it may be easier to wade in the stream if the water is low and the bottom hard.

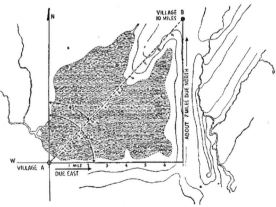

Figure 6. Jungle navigation by dead reckoning. The simplest case in which the course comprises 2 legs or elements.

k. The easiest way to travel through the jungle is by water if there are no rapids. If a boat cannot be obtained from the local inhabitants, a raft can be made. However, water routes are very vulnerable to ambush.

l. Because it is seldom possible to maintain direction in the jungle by landmarks, it is necessary to know how to navigate by the process of "dead reckoning." The process is similar to that used by a ship captain attempting to reach a small island in the middle of the ocean, if he were forced to sail other than a straight course and if he were unable, because of dense fogs, day and night, to determine his position from time to time by celestial observation. The process is to determine and plot on paper the direction and distance traveled on each leg of a journey. As an example, assume that it is desired to travel from village A to village B. The map indicates that the azimuth of the line from village A to village B is 45°; that is, village B is exactly northeast of village A (see fig. 6). The map also indicates that the distance between the two villages is ten miles. Obviously the shortest path between the two villages is the straight line on an azimuth of 45°. But assume that it is not possible to follow this line because of a large swamp. To skirt the swamp it is necessary to leave village A on an azimuth of 90°; that is, due east from the village. The traveller continues due east from village A for a distance of seven miles before he finds dry land on which he can turn north toward village B. He then sits down and plots his position on his map. He sees that village B must be due north of his present position and at a distance of about seven miles. He therefore turns due north and follows this line directly to village B. This is a simple case, as the course comprised only two legs, or elements. In actual practice, many more legs will often be involved, but the principle used is the same. The direction and distance of each leg of the journey is plotted on the map as a continuous line extending from the starting point. The position at any time is known, therefore, and the direction and distance from that point to the destination can be determined. (See fig. 7.)

m. There are two methods of determining distance by other than direct measurement. These are by pacing and by intervals of time. Pacing means counting the steps or strides (two steps) taken, the number of steps, or strides, per hundred yards being known. The average length of a step will be different for each man and it will vary for each individual depending upon whether the terrain is level or hilly, dry or muddy, wooded or open. This can be determined only by a man actually walking a known distance over each type of terrain at his normal gait and counting his steps or strides. With practice, considerable accuracy can be obtained by pacing. Another method

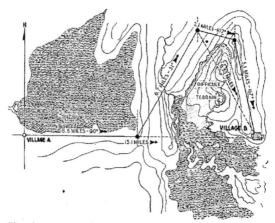

Figure 7. Jungle navigation by dead reckoning. Case involving by-passing of two obstructions, in which the course comprises 4 legs or elements.

of measuring distance for general jungle navigation is by time. No rules can be laid down for determining exactly the distance a man will travel through the jungle in a given time, however, this rate will seldom exceed one mile per hour. By using this figure as a guide, the rate of movement over varied terrain can be estimated with reasonable accuracy. By a check of the length of time of travel, the distance travelled can be calculated. Such checking and estimating will not enable a man to walk 10 or 15 miles from one village to another and come out of the jungle exactly at the second village. The method should, however, enable him to come close enough to the second village to encounter the trails leading to it.

n. If neither a compass nor a watch is available, the sun must be used for determining both time and direction. This method is, however, very inaccurate. On approximately 22 June, the sun is 23½° north of the Equator; that is, over the Tropic of Cancer. Within accuracy limits suitable for jungle navigation, it will appear from any point within the Torrid Zone to rise 25° north of due east and set 25° north of due west. On approximately 22 December, the sun is 23½° south of the Equator; that is, over the Tropic of Capricorn, and from within the Torrid Zone will appear to rise 25° south of due east and to set 25°

south of due west. On approximately 21 March and 23 September, the sun is directly over the Equator, and from any point within the Torrid Zone will appear to rise in the true east and set in the true west. With these few dates in mind it is possible to estimate the position of the rising and setting sun for any time of the year. It is then possible to estimate directions from the sun until about 1000 and after 1400. The sun may thus be used as a general guide in walking a line in any desired direction. The higher the sun above the horizon, the more difficult it will be to estimate direction by its location; during and about mid-day, its location will not serve as a practical guide to determine direction.

o. In attempting to use a shadow to determine direction, it is desirable to use an improvised plumb bob. A rock or piece of wood tied to the end of a 3- or 4-foot length of thin vine will serve the purpose. This method is unsatisfactory when the sun is nearly directly overhead.

p. Telling time by the sun is merely a matter of estimating divisions of the sun's arc overhead. For instance, half of the arc would put the sun directly overhead and the time would be noon. One quarter of the arc would indicate 0900, and three quarters of the arc, 1500. This is based on the assumption that the sun rises at exactly 0600 and sets at exactly 1800 when observed from any point in the Torrid Zone, which is not precisely true. The assumption is accurate enough, however, for practical purposes.

q. Another method of determining direction in the jungle is by the direction of prevailing winds. This is an exceedingly doubtful procedure and should be used only in an emergency. Although tropical areas are characterized by winds which blow regularly from one direction during a particular season, topography, local storms, and the trees themselves affect wind direction, making it impossible to determine directions from the wind with any degree of accuracy except by averages based upon observations covering a period of several days. Factors close to the ground do much to influence the direction of the wind, but reasonably reliable estimates of direction can be made from observing the direction of the wind over water.

Camouflage in Jungle Warfare
from *Notes from Theatres of War* 17

1. Background

(a) Jungle war suggests a background of dense equatorial vegetation, but the Eastern theatre of war contains a variety of tropical backgrounds against which it may be necessary to fight. The following notes are compiled from reports from various sources, mainly unofficial, with the object of giving a general picture; but it must be borne in mind that what is true of one place may not necessarily be true of another.

(b) *Types of country likely to be encountered:*—

(i) *Jungle.*—In jungle which has never been cleared (primary jungle) visibility is from 20 to 30 yds. Growth is thinner on the top of the hills. Small impassable swamps are formed where streams have been blocked. Visibility is even shorter in jungle which has been cleared and overgrown (secondary jungle). Growth is thicker but not so high. Frequent rivers and streams are met and the jungle is very thick on their banks. Lateral movement becomes difficult, which encourages infiltration. Tracks for men and mules may have to be cut through bamboo jungle. Jungle vegetation is blue green in colour compared with European greens and is very dark in tone. There is plenty of black.

(ii) *Cultivation.*—There are large areas cultivated, for example:—

(*a*) *Rubber plantations.*—These grow in straight lines 20–30 ft apart. Visibility 100–300 yds. There are frequent tracks for MT.

(*b*) *Paddy fields.*—In the dry season the cracked ground and bunds (embankments, often carrying roads and paths) make marching difficult. Bunds have to be cleared to let MT pass. When wet, paddy fields are often knee deep (or deeper) in mud. Progress is slow and exhausting.

(*c*) There are areas such as the jungle in parts of Assam which are notable for absence of tree cover. Waist high scrub is usually the only form of cover. Some areas consist of many small scrub covered hills. Tracks and smooth surface show up very clearly and spoil may be very light. In summer roads are inches deep in dust.

(*d*) The monsoon (or corresponding rainy season) provides a respite when attack and patrol are hampered and activity hidden. Afterwards fresh vegetation grows on tracks or spoil and texture is restored. It may be necessary to discontinue the use of camouflage nets during the monsoon.

2. Ground view.—The closer the jungle the closer the range at which concealment is necessary. Details not normally considered become important—slight shine on a weapon, a wrist watch, light rolled socks, small signs which distinguish an officer from ORs.

Where scrub thins out on the ground long range automatic weapons will have greater scope. Clearances may be made for fields of fire, but these will be very obvious. Defensive positions become subject to artillery fire and air observation and attack.

3. Air view.—Aircraft flying over a dreary expanse of scrub or an endless sea of jungle will automatically follow roads and tracks—anything of interest on or near them will attract them, but a winding track among high trees is very hard to follow. A clearing in continuous jungle will be as noticeable as isolated cover in open country. Consequently activity on L of C, dumps, staging camps, etc, is very liable to attack. The air view over treed jungle will be in the form of the vertical photograph and near vertical visual. The low oblique view only becomes effective in areas of scrub.

A report from the Pacific states that the Japanese send over recce aircraft after first light to pick targets for escorted dive bombers, which come within 48 hours; possibly photographs are taken. The report recommends siting of dumps and camps on a hillside up a narrow re-entrant away from the main L of C, and that in forward areas sleeping accommodation, offices, and stores be dug into hillsides and then concealed.

4. Individual concealment.—The following items suggest the type of equipment used in this type of fighting:—

(a) *Clothing.*—All clothing must be dark.

Head.—Soft headgear of indeterminate shape is best (*e.g.*, beret type) which will not fall off. The topee is conspicuous, clumsy, and fragile. The steel helmet, noisy and heavy; where it is used a black cover or black garnish is needed.

Body.—Dark olive green battle dress. Anklets or short puttees with trousers.

(b) *Equipment.*—All equipment should be dark in colour.

Field glasses should be carried slung under arm without case. Case is an officer mark. A small dark green canvas cover will keep out dust and prevent shine.

(c) *Face darkener.*—Apart from the necessity of being inconspicuous, it is important to darken the faces of officers working with native troops. A black face stain which will be wholesome to the skin is required. It need not be easily removable; it must be long-lasting, must not interfere with sweating, and must not be removed easily by water.

(d) *Personal net.*—A personal net is of great value in close range fighting. In one division nets have been made locally with a mesh large enough to take scrim or head vegetation, twigs or creeper. Live flat-leafed vegetation cannot be used in the sun since it dies quickly.

(e) *Behaviour.*—Men have to be taught to hold their fire and only to fire at the body when they are absolutely certain—never at noise or lights. The enemy will try every trick to draw fire and locate positions. Noise is a great danger. Men must lie up in complete silence without talking or coughing.

Care must be taken not to move undergrowth which will be seen or will make a noise.

Intensive training in necessary in fieldcraft: use of shadow, ground and cover, firing round cover, crawling.

5. Concealment from the air.—Siting, track planning, concealment discipline, removal of spoil, and use of nets are as important as in N. Europe. The background is often even darker. Smoke and fires need careful control.

MT should be parked off the road, although it is rarely possible to go more than a few yards. Flat leafed foliage must not be cut for MT or infantry position, since it soon turns yellow. Hides for vehicles can be made by pulling together small trees or bushes and tying them together with rope made on the spot from local creeper. Tracks over low scrub are easily visible since the brushwood is flattened.

A track plan should follow trees or bare ground.

Road dust in summer will be especially obvious against dark foliage or scrub. MT should be stopped short of HQ.

MT with superstructure removed has been found easier to conceal. Tops should in any case be painted black.

Troops on L of C tend to take off their shirts to work and so attract attention.

"Meals, mules, and washing" were said to show most. Pack animals on the move are difficult to see on rough ground, but are more obvious than men. Light coloured loads and covers are a danger. Where standings have existed for some time a serious mess is made and if tree cover is inadequate, overhead cover must be added. In one case permanent standings had been cut into the hillside and roofed over with brushwood.

AA.—When thick roadless jungle makes large scale movement slow, Bofors in either AA or A tk or dual role are likely to remain in position for some time. They will have to occupy such open spaces as are available or have clearings made. Where there is danger of AFVs it may be difficult to get good ground concealment and field of fire for AA role. It is likely that AA role will demand a 360 degrees arc of fire. This is not incompatible with good concealment in scrub, but in treed jungle may give away other troops. Near villages AA LMG and Bofors may be disguised as haystacks, huts, etc.

Materials.—Natural materials—creeper, foliage, leaf cover of bamboo, etc., bamboo cane for supports and framework.

Salvage textile materials rot very quickly.

The net is very valuable. Sisal nets probably last longest. Nets must always be rot-proof.

The new garnish is satisfactory. Colour of garnish should be black and green. In thick jungle brown is not required. Knots or bow-ties should be used, strip garnish is less suitable. Patch and knot nets with black patches are also suitable. Black is a safe jungle colour. The shrimp net is unlikely to be of any use.

Display.—Display to suggest greater strength that is actually present should be easy in country where it is invariably difficult to gauge strength. Good use may be made of smoke, domestic activity, AA fire, tracks in the open, or paths and field of fire cut through the jungle.

KNOWING THE ENEMY

Due to the quick and successful advances of the IJA in 1941–1942 they had a reputation of being 'supermen' in the jungle. They used a number of ruses that misled the troops in these early defeats (pp. 131–135). Contributing to this reputation was the fact that the Japanese saw surrender as dishonourable and as a result often fought until the last man standing. It took time to destroy this myth, through training and such successful actions of the Australian Army at Milne Bay in New Guinea in 1942 and the first Chindit operation.

The first pamphlet on the Japanese forces was produced by American forces. It was written by Colonel Francis Brink entitled *Japanese Tactical Methods* in 1941. It was quickly adopted by Australian, British and Indian troops and reprinted in India the same year. From then on, information about the Imperial Japanese Army and their tactical methods was continually disseminated by the War Department in Washington through publications like the *Intelligence Bulletin* and *Tactical and Technical Trends*; in *Current Reports from Overseas* and *Notes from Theatres of War* produced by the War Office in London; and the large amount of training pamphlets and memoranda produced by GHQ India.

A copy of *Soldier's Guide to the Japanese Army*, published by the US Military Intelligence service in 1944 was distributed to every squad/platoon, and the frontispiece urged soldiers to pass their copy on so all could read it. It covered how Japanese soldiers were trained, equipped and armed, how the army operated, and summaries of its tactics on the offensive, defensive, in the jungle, and with artillery and tanks.

Soldier's Guide to the Japanese Army

JUNGLE WARFARE

Offensive

Japanese successes in the early phase of the war were won largely because their troops were especially prepared and trained for operations in jungle terrain. In such warfare the weakness of their artillery and their comparative lack of motorized transport did not tell so decisively against them as would have been the case had operations been conducted in open country. And the ability of Japanese troops to live off the land compensated, to some extent, for weaknesses in their army supply system.

Japanese offensive doctrine naturally is modified somewhat when it is necessary to adapt infantry to jungle conditions. The need for adequate reconnaissance is emphasized even more strongly than for other types of combat. Good security for front, rear, and flanks is stressed. The importance of effective patrolling, for both offensive and defensive purposes, likewise receives emphasis in Japanese tactical manuals and studies. As in open warfare, envelopments are favorite tactical maneuvers, but attacks which aim at point penetration are commonly utilized, especially after an enemy strong point or artillery position has been liquidated by a night attack or raid.

Reconnaissance in the jungle normally is conducted by picked and specially trained troops. The function of reconnaissance patrols is to gain contact with the enemy and develop his position. Ordinarily such patrols will comprise five to ten men who are provided with compasses, portable radio, and mapping equipment.

Advancing Japanese forces in the jungle usually move along trails in single-column formation. Where no trail is available the march is made along suitable terrain and the column is preceded by a chopping group to cut the dense foliage. Engineers also are sent ahead when formidable natural or artificial obstacles to the advance are anticipated. The rate of march is about five-eighths of a mile every two hours; from four to six miles ordinarily are covered in a day. The rate of advance actually is limited by the speed with which the heavy weapons can be transported. Direction is maintained by compass and, even in jungle country, the Japanese are well provided with fairly accurate maps. Special care is exercised in crossing clearings in the jungle; often these are traversed by leaps and bounds, and every precaution is taken when the advancing column enters areas where hostile artillery concentrations may be brought down.

In the jungle, as in other types of terrain, the main body is preceded by an advance guard. If the Japanese unit is of battalion strength, ordinarily the advance will be one company; if a company constitutes the total force, one platoon is used for this purpose.

If contact is made with the enemy, the Japanese advance guard immediately informs the commander of the main body and attempts to liquidate hostile resistance. If this cannot be accomplished, the advance guard deploys or simulates deployment and tries to locate the enemy's flanks and heavy weapons. This is considered essential, since in the meantime the main force deploys and moves against one or both flanks. The objective is to strike the enemy deep in his flanks or in the rear. It is believed that final victory must be won in hand-to-hand combat. Tactics are fundamentally those generally prescribed by the Japanese for a meeting engagement, and even small units follow this basic pattern in actions of this type.

When the enemy is encountered in deployed defense, the Japanese may resort to either of two basic methods. In one procedure they conduct a demonstration along the enemy front with much promiscuous firing of automatic weapons and even firecrackers to simulate strength. While this holding action is occurring along the front, the main force deploys toward one or both flanks to initiate the usual envelopment maneuver.

When the alternative method is employed, the Japanese "feel out" soft spots in the enemy line. Special efforts are made to locate hostile heavy weapons. Often this is done by opening up with light machine-gun fire until the enemy opens fire in reply and thus reveals his location. As soon as the heavy weapons are located with sufficient accuracy, the Japanese bring heavy mortar fire to bear on them. Usually the mortar concentration hits the hostile positions just as the advancing Japanese reach assault distance. The assault then is delivered on a narrow front, if necessary by two or more assault echelons.

Jungle terrain affords a maximum opportunity to utilize the effective Japanese infiltration tactics. As a holding attack is delivered frontally to confuse and distract the enemy, patrols move to the enemy flanks. The personnel of these patrols are armed with light machine guns and grenades, and are provided with compact rations comprising rice, condensed foods, and vitamin tablets. The patrols wriggle through presumably impenetrable jungle to get around the enemy's flanks and into his rear areas. Unless the enemy has cleared areas of fire, such infiltrations of his positions are virtually impossible to stop. Sometimes, after reaching suitable positions in the enemy rear areas, the Japanese infiltration patrols dig in, or they may combine with other similar units to build up a force that may be truly decisive.

Snipers almost invariably are sent out; each Japanese squad has two men normally assigned to sniping missions. These have for their fundamental purpose distraction of the enemy from his main tactical effort. The patience of these snipers is almost incredible. They have been known to lie in wait for three days to fire a single shot, and they have no hesitation in firing even when they are certain to be killed immediately by retaliatory fire. They are adroitly camouflaged and selected their positions with great skill. Fortunately, however, their marksmanship is so poor, that they rarely are effective at ranges much beyond 50 yards.

Japanese infantry support weapons are employed with daring on the offense, although the restricted fields of their machine-gun fire in the jungle preclude maximum exploitation of their potentialities. The machine guns usually are sited well forward in pairs, in positions whence they can support the front-line infantry. They are emplaced as secretly as possible and open fire when the maximum surprise effect can be obtained. If antitank guns are available and are not needed for their primary antitank role, they fire upon hostile infantry. Battalion and regimental guns are sited well forward, and are used in the jungle primarily against heavy machine guns.

Defensive
Japanese defense in the jungle follows the general doctrinal concept applicable, in Japanese opinion, to all defensive situations. Defensive lines are expected to bend with the blow of the hostile assault until an opportunity arises to deliver a hard and sudden counterblow to regain the initiative, and even lead to decisive victory.

As in other areas, Japanese defense in the jungle makes use of forward and main defense positions. The forward position has for its main purpose prevention of enemy surprise of the main body. When contact is made with an advancing enemy, the forward defense line may either withdraw or remain in concealment to harass the enemy. In the event the latter course is adopted, great care is taken by the Japanese to avoid premature disclosure of the location of their automatic weapons. In small unit actions the forward defense will be entrusted to a few snipers who will warn the main body of the enemy's approach. Often snipers will permit the enemy to pass through so they subsequently can be harassed from the rear. At the main line of resistance the

Japanese attempt to achieve tactical surprise by withholding their fire until the last possible moment. Often they do not open up until the enemy's advance troops have come so close that his artillery and mortar fires have been lifted. On occasion the defensive fire has not been opened until opposing forces were within ten yards of the Japanese positions. If the attacking force is larger, however, it will be fired upon when within about 50 yards of the defensive line. Japanese automatic weapons are well sited for defense and ordinarily open fire as soon as the enemy enters their lanes of fire. Machine-gun fire is delivered in great volume and is supplement by grenade dischargers and mortars from positions just to the rear of the front line. Certain automatic weapons may remain silent, if not immediately threatened by the enemy attack, and will later open surprise fire.

Japanese Ruses
from *Notes from Theatres of War* 19: Burma 1943/1944

(Compiled by Headquarters, Fourteenth Army)

Foreword by the Army Commander

"Here is a list of the ruses the Jap has used against us up to now. He is not very imaginative, and in everything he does he goes on repeating himself; so he will probably try them against you again. Be ready and don't be had for a mug.

"You are cleverer than the Jap, you've got more imagination, and you are better than he is in the jungle. Don't be content merely to laugh at his clumsy ruses; think up some hot ones of your own and put them over on him. Don't make his mistake of doing the same thing in the same way too often. Keep him guessing and he'll soon get the jitters."

Use of British and Indian languages

On many fronts, the Japanese have used the language of the troops opposing them with the object of persuading them to act on false orders, encouraging them to surrender, or pin-pointing their positions. Although the enemy's accent is often bad, it has sometimes been good enough to deceive our troops. Some typical examples are given in the following paragraphs.

The enemy have been heard to call out in English, "Where is the CO?" or shout an order such as, "No. 1 Section, cease fire."

In Burma, the names of units, as well as the names of officers and men, have often been called out in Urdu with the intention of confusing our troops.

At night, a voice has been heard to shout in English, "No. 1 Section, by the right—advance," which is followed by a burst of fire but no movement; or a voice may call out in bad Urdu, "Do number section, hamla kya," at which there is a burst of fire from the enemy, but again no movement.

During an attack by Bengali-speaking troops, a voice was heard calling out to them in their own language, "Don't shoot, don't shoot, we are (naming the battalion concerned). Where are you?" (The answer was a burst of automatic fire.)

In another theatre, the Japanese have put down a smoke screen at night on positions occupied by our forces and charged, shouting, in English, "Gas".

Use of wounded and dead bodies as decoys

The Japanese sometimes leave the bodies of British and Indian soldiers, who have become casualties in previous attacks, lying on tracks or in front of their positions, and covered by machine guns. When our troops make attempts to recover the bodies heavy fire is opened at close range. Bodies have also been seen propped up against trees or in front of the enemy's positions, apparently with the object of discovering other advancing troops. Again, a party of Japanese once lay up near one of our wounded in the hope of ambushing any troops who went out to rescue him.

Use of dummies

In the Chin Hills and elsewhere Japanese positions have been seen manned by dummy figures with dummy weapons, with the twofold object of drawing our fire and giving a false impression of their own strength. The dummies, dressed in correct uniform with steel helmets, are often very realistic.

Use of animals

The Japanese sometimes tether dogs near their positions. They beat and maltreat the animals so that they bark and howl whenever they hear anyone approaching, and thus give the enemy warning of the present of our patrols.

Small enemy patrols have advanced towards our positions driving cows before them. On one occasion they were heard striking a wooden clapper which they had removed from the neck of a cow.

In Northern Burma two Japanese were once seen driving a mule ahead of them with long bamboo poles. They were advancing up a little used jungle track, and the mule's lot clearly was to spring any booby trap that might have been laid on the path.

Use of noise

In all theatres the Japanese have made much use of noise to deceive and demoralize our troops. For example, bullets that explode on impact have been fired over the heads of our troops (the sound of explosions coming from behind and from the flanks is apt to deceive inexperienced troops into thinking that they have been surrounded).

To give the impression of greater fire power, the Japanese have been known to imitate the noise of machine guns either with wooden rattles or by beating two bamboo sticks together.

Chinese crackers thrown into our positions at night, mortar bombs bursting with a loud explosion, and rattling rifle bolts are some of the devices that have been employed to give an impression of strength and lower the morale of our troops in the hope of causing them to withdraw prematurely.

From the South-West Pacific it has been reported that the Japanese have kept absolute silence while they have been moving forward to take up their positions, but that when they have reached their objective they have made as much noise as they could in order to suggest that they were a larger force that they actually were. Similarly, enemy troops making a frontal advance have created a noise in order to cover the silent move towards the flank of the main attacking force.

Use of uniforms and civilian clothing

Japanese patrols have been seen wearing British uniforms and Gurkha style hats with the object of deceiving our troops into believing that they were friendly patrols.

During attempts to infiltrate through our positions the enemy have sometimes adopted the dress of the local villagers; and in Burma, Japanese have been seen wearing *lungis* and the yellow robes of priests.

Use of our own troops as decoys

In New Guinea, Japanese advancing against our positions would sometimes turn and flee when they met machine gun fire. With their usual cry of "After the bastards", the Australians would rush forward with bayonets fixed. Almost immediately the fleeing Japanese threw themselves to the ground and the Australians ran into withering machine gun fire from the Japanese rear.

The enemy once made an attempt to draw our troops into the same trap in the Chin Hills, when Japanese were seen running away during an attack, shouting, screaming, and displaying every sign of panic. But our troops were wise to the ruse, and resisted the temptation to walk into a possible ambush.

Another trick which the Japanese often attempted was to cut our signal lines and then set an ambush for the repair party, or wait for it with snipers. (The enemy is not the only one to carry out this form of ambush, and on several occasions our troops have used the same method to ensnare him.)

The Japanese take infinite pains to encourage their enemy to disclose the locations of their artillery and machine gun positions. Besides their usual tactics of firing verey lights, flashing lamps, creating noises near our positions, and firing indiscriminate bursts from machine guns, they are sometimes prepared to risk casualties in order to draw our fire.

Civilians forcibly employed to allay suspicion

Quite apart from the use they make of "Fifth Columnists", the Japanese do not hesitate to compel the local population to help them. They often employ villagers as guides, and in the Arakan natives have been posted on tracks to watch and give warning of the approach of our patrols. Again, civilians have been forced to drive private cars to bridges that we have prepared for demolition so that Japanese hidden in the cars could shoot up the troops guarding them. During the 1942 campaign in Burma the enemy carried out moves in daylight covered by Burmans whom they compelled to drive bullock carts in which Japanese and their arms were concealed.

Deception with artillery fire

When our troops have been advancing supported by a creeping artillery barrage, the Japanese have more than once put down artillery fire immediately in front of or amongst our troops with the object of creating the impression that our shells were falling short. The intention here is to destroy the confidence of our troops in their own artillery, and discourage them from pressing home their attack.

Booby traps and decoys

Besides using the usual rattling tin cans and laying trip-wires across paths and in front of their positions, the Japanese show considerable ingenuity in planning booby paths and decoys. Articles of equipment and clothing found in areas frequented by our patrols, or where the enemy has been contacted, may be so wired that they will detonate a grenade when they are touched; or a fallen tree may be so placed across a road or jungle path that it will explode a mine when it is removed.

Sometimes a number of empty cartridge cases or articles of equipment have been left strewn about on a track with the object of tempting our troops to remove them and thus disclose to the enemy the fact that we have recently passed through the area. Alternatively, this ruse is used to encourage our troops to halt and gather around the spot where the articles are found and, in doing so, provide the target for an ambush.

While searches were being made for enemy documents in the South-West Pacific area, it was discovered that the Japanese were using a new type of booby trap with buried documents. A hole, partly filled in, was found containing three haversacks full of documents and, underneath them, mortar bombs set to explode if they were struck by a spade or other heavy instrument.

Deceit

The enemy often use small parties of men to move about his area and show themselves from time to time in order to confuse our observers and present a picture of greater strength than he actually possesses. This ruse is often adapted to create the impression that all his dug positions are occupied, whereas in fact he has not the resources to man more than a few of them.

Pretending to surrender, Japanese have approached out positions with both hands above their heads and, when only a short distance away, have tossed a grenade towards our troops from each raised hand, Similarly, they have used the white flag of truce to enable them to approach close to our forces in safety.

In order to draw our artillery fire the Japanese have sometimes sent patrols to light fires in an area some distance from their own positions. The smoke rising from these fires, by giving the impression that enemy troops are located in that area, encourages our artillery to open fire and disclose their positions.

Use of civilians to give warning of patrols

When our patrols have reached certain villages on the west bank of the Chindwin they have noticed that some of the villagers have at once moved down to the river and made a pretence of washing red *lungis*, which they then place on the bank to dry. The villagers have been ordered by the Japanese to do this "washing" in order to given warning to their OPs on the east bank of the presence of our patrols. After the patrols have left the area of the village, the information is conveyed to the east bank by a display of white clothing.

In the Arakan, villagers have been placed by the Japanese in front of their posts to act as sentries and give warning of the approach of British patrols. They have been forced to "co-operate" in this way under threat of reprisals against their families.

False orders issued by wireless

In the Arakan, false orders have been issued by wireless. One of our units, which had been ordered to move to a certain area, received a bogus wireless message which cancelled the first instruction and ordered it to proceed to an entirely different area. (In the main, however, the Japanese seldom attempted to pass false orders; their aim was chiefly to cause delay to our communications and confusion among our operators.)

CHAPTER 3
LEARNING THE LESSONS

essons were continually learnt by all units and formations in India, Burma and South West Pacific theatre. In India, the doctrine of *The Jungle Book* was added to through the *Army in India Training Memoranda* (AITMs, see also pp. 62–66) that encapsulated lessons from the battle front and disseminated throughout the Indian Army. Thus doctrine was both a top-down and bottom-up process with the doctrine produced centrally and continually added to after battle experience from unit level upwards. Added to which within the divisions, the Indian Army in all theatres of war produced training instructions that continually updated training and tactics from battle experience.

Similar to 23rd Indian Division, 7th Indian Division had time to learn from the Second Arakan campaign as the divisional commanding officer, General Frank Messervy, stated in his first training directive: 'Now that the Division is coming into reserve after 7 months in the line the opportunity will be taken to polish up certain lines of training which need constant attention' such as weapons training, drill and preparation of defences for monsoon garrisons (7th Indian Division Commander's Training Directive No. 1, 5 April 1944, TNA, WO 172/4290). In addition each brigade within the division was to set up a committee to study the lessons of the campaign. The establishing paper asked for comments on the principles in the training manuals, the s, divisional operational and training notes with particular reference to patrolling, ambushes, night operations and generally attack and defence.

Similarly after the successful defensive battles of Kohima and Imphal, the Fourteenth Army was by no means perfect by the summer of 1944, but now had the upper hand over the Japanese: 7th Indian Division's 2nd Training Instruction commented:

> Although we have now behind us 10 months of operational experience, that does not mean that we are by any means perfect in battle. On the contrary, the wastage in junior leaders and the absorptions of a large number of reinforcements have decreased our battle efficiency. But, with that experience to guide us, we can now in a comparatively short time not only regain the efficiency of last autumn but greatly – surpass it. *(7th Indian Division Training Instruction No. 2, 3 July 1944, TNA, WO 172/4290)*

Thus the division needed to study and analyse the lessons from the Arakan and the experiences from Kohima and Imphal and apply them to training. This was achieved through company training, the training of junior leaders and individual training. Company training was through discussions on cloth or sand models, Tactical Exercises Without Troops and exercises. The training of junior leaders was seen a priority as success in battle depended on good leadership with individual training ranging from weapon training to field hygiene.

The Fourteenth Army prepared for the next phase of the fighting and a culture of training and continually learning lessons was instilled in 7th Indian Division and across the Indian Army. Lessons were also learned by the US Marines and US Army fighting on Guadalcanal Island and in New Guinea. In 1942, Lieutenant Colonel Russell Reader interviewed fifty-nine officers and other ranks on Guadalcanal, and these interviews were published as *Notes on Jungle Warfare from the U.S. Marines and U.S. Infantry on Guadalcanal Island* and distributed at the Infantry School. As in India, he noted the importance of junior leadership, the importance of patrolling but there were differences as the Americans did not undertake night operations whereas the Indian Army underwent night training in all theatres. In New Guinea the need for training and experience was paramount (as demonstrated by 'Bill' Slim's quote in the introduction). *Combat Lessons* stated:

> The operations amply illustrated the need for thorough training of units and individuals in scouting and patrolling, They also proved, however, that there is no substitute for experience. It is therefore logical that in addition to training, every opportunity should be taken to give our troops actual experience in scouting and patrolling against the enemy.

Battle Instructions for Jungle Fighting
23 Indian Division

Part I – General

<u>Offensive Spirit</u>

The offensive spirit in attack and defence within the division was with very few exceptions, excellent. Among certain units, however, fighting patrols were definitely not imbued with the determination to get close and kill. In the jungle it is not difficult for a patrol to carry out a surprise raid or ambush and get away unscathed. There must be an improvement.

The biggest test of a leader is his ability to weigh up all the factors and decide correctly whether to go on or not. Whenever in doubt, the bold policy is best. Our own difficulties are so apparent, that we forget those of the enemy. When making your decision, never forget all the difficulties with which the enemy will have to contend; some of these difficulties are obvious; others you can merely surmise. There have been a few occasions when our own difficulties have been allowed to assume undue proportions. Do not take counsel of your fears.

<u>Information</u>

A commander cannot make a plan without information. Every officer and man must be made to realise the importance firstly of obtaining information and secondly passing it back quickly. Intelligence personnel the whole way up the chain must ensure that their respective commanders are being kept fully informed, and don't forget to pass the information to the flanks.

The importance of securing documents and sending them back immediately must be impressed on all ranks. In every campaign against the Japanese so far, the numbers of Japanese have always been very considerably exaggerated. The Jap mixes up sub units continually, and the presence of a platoon does not prove the presence of a company, nor does an identified company prove the presence of the battalion. In the jungle too, a few men can be made to represent many. Furthermore the Jap always takes considerable risks in order to maintain the initiative by offensive action and will continue the offensive even when units are 50 per cent or more below strength owing to casualties. These factors must be kept in mind when studying intelligence reports.

Know your enemy. The study of Japanese methods and organisation must be continuous both during training and in action, and we must learn to profit by Jap weaknesses, which are fortunately many. In order that the many shall benefit from the experience of the few, subordinate commanders must send back early reports of Jap methods and equipment; these are particularly required if the Jap adopts anything new, but it is also very valuable to know that the same old methods are being employed. The Japs have stuck to their same stereotyped tactics, although they did introduce a few new weapons such as flame throwers. These were not effective. But we must be prepared for changes, in particular a more lavish use of anti-tank and anti-personnel mines.

Observation in the jungle is always difficult. Full use must therefore be made of air photographs, particularly in planning an advance or attack. In our next operations air photographs should be available in greater quantities and at shorter notice. It is most important that all officers should take every opportunity for training in the use of air photographs. As many vacancies as possible will be obtained on the Shillong Photo Interpretation course.

More use must be made of infantry observation posts, and a much higher standard of training in observation is necessary.

In the dry season water will be the ruling factor when planning an advance or attack. Detailed up-to-date information regarding available water supplies must be obtained and marked on a water supply map. This information will be acquired by patrols and from local inhabitants. Plans must ensure sufficient water for our own troops and endeavour to deny water to the enemy.

The rapid sending back of documents, identifications etc, has been good. But on the whole, brigade and battalion Intelligence officers did not do their task well, in that they did not ensure a regular flow of complete and accurate sitreps, nor did they disseminate sufficient information to battalions. Commanders must get on to the training of their B.I.Os. The fact that a Brigade Major has passed an item of information over the phone to the G.S.O.II does not absolve the B.I.O. from including that item in his sitrep.

Patrols

Jap patrolling has been of a very low standard, particularly with regard to protective patrolling to prevent surprise. We were thus able to carry out many surprise attacks, and we must exploit this advantage to the full in the future.

In order to prevent Jap attacks from taking us by surprise, small recce patrols will operate over the whole area between us and the Japs and all round the Japs. These patrols will consist normally of only two or three men and never more than a section and will not disclose their presence. Our protective patrol screens have on the whole been very good. There has, however, been more than one occasion of careless handing over, with the result that ground, which the commander believed to be covered by patrols, was not in fact being covered. The handing over of patrol tasks must be carefully checked by the commander responsible for sending out patrols.

Fighting patrols, varying from a platoon to a company in strength will be used frequently to fight for information and to ambush and harass the enemy.

Patrols must operate on a definite plan. There were several cases of patrol programmes being badly planned, or not planned at all. All commanders must plan their patrol programmes with care and issue detailed orders for patrol leaders. It will be necessary at times for Brigade Commanders personally to brief a patrol leader. The patrol leaders must then make their detailed plans. Separate instructions on patrolling will be issued.

<u>Vigilance</u>
In spite of all that has been written and spoken on the need for vigilance at all times, more than one occasion has occurred in which we have been surprised through pure carelessness. When in and area of operations you must always be alert with your weapon in your hand ready to fire. Parties at work, patrols at rest, etc., must be protected by listening posts. When travelling in M.T. the hood must be down and men ready to fire to both flanks. The Jap is very careless and has suffered many unnecessary casualties as a result. Let us profit by their lesson. Any leader whose men become casualties through lack of vigilance, must accept the responsibility for the needless loss of life, for this loss is due to his carelessness or slackness and to no other causes. On training exercises, men must be vigilant at all times; never allow a single let-up. Vigilance must be so instilled into the men that on service it will be instinctive. Nevertheless, ensure the maximum rest for your men by reducing the number of listening posts to the essential minimum.

<u>Fire Control</u>
Good fire control is essential, and particularly when any unit or sub unit is in an isolated position, where replenishment of ammunition will be difficult. The Jap uses many ruses to draw our fire; these have been published in War Information Circulars and Training Instructions; they must be studied by all officers, and explained to the men.

Don't overdo fire control. Don't allow a Jap to inspect the position and not fire at him for fear of giving away the position. But fire to kill. Let our slogan be "one bullet – one Jap". Consider the reasons for fire control and use your common sense. Don't spare ammunition if you can spare lives by using it.

Fire control is necessary, not only to economise ammunition, but far more important to preserve silence. If the enemy send parties out at night to draw our fire, don't shoot at them, unless you can see to kill, but lob a grenade amongst them. This method gives little away and causes casualties. The value of grenades both in attack and defence was proved again and again – sometimes even a sandbag full per man being necessary.

Fire Support

In all types of operation use the maximum possible fire support, artillery, tanks, air and small arms. If 100 shells will save one man's life, they are worth while, provided it doesn't mean that you will be short for a more important task.

Columns carrying out wide turning movements must watch their ammunition expenditure carefully, but make the maximum use of support and of supply of ammunition by air to enable you to provide effective fire support. O.P.'s from the artillery units with the main force should accompany the column, so that they can support the flanking column as soon as they get within range.

Snipers

In spite of all that has been written about Jap snipers, there are still frequent reports of attacks being held up by them. Why? Because no adequate plans for dealing with them have been made and because troops had not been properly trained. The Japs use these snipers – often on suicidal tasks – in every phase of battle. You must be continually on your guard against them. Never plan any advance that does not include detailed arrangements for dealing with snipers.

Thought and Sweat

"Sweat saves blood". We have learnt this lesson well and saved ourselves casualties on many occasions. We now realise the value of our slogan "DIG or DIE". Blood is saved not only by digging, but also by the physical effort expended in movement – deep patrolling – changing position – approach by the difficult but unexpected route, etc. This lesson we have learnt also, but don't forget the value of alternative defensive positions.

Even more important, "Thought saves sweat and blood". Jungle fighting is largely a battle of wits. All ranks, and junior leaders in particular, must be alert and keep their wits about them. On one occasion a small party found themselves surrounded on top of the hill. So they rolled down unprimed grenades on to the Japs and while the Japs' heads were down, ran clean through them and so escaped. How many of your junior leaders would have thought of that one?

Cross-country Movement
We carried out many successful cross-country movements and have learnt many lessons which are worth enumerating:–

(a) Practically no country is impassable to men determined to reach their objective.

(b) Moves nearly always take longer than anticipated. In planning a turning movement, there must always be a time reserve.

(c) Mules can be got over very difficult country given sufficient time.

(d) It always seems to be the wireless mule that goes over the khud. Therefore carry some, if not all, W/T sets on man packs. Reliefs will be necessary, and the men's packs should be carried on mules.

(e) The value of artillery was proved more than once. We took mountain guns to most places, and on occasion at least by superhuman efforts got 25 pounders as a complete surprise behind the enemy.

(f) Porters, even of indifferent quality, were invaluable. Apart from carrying loads forward, they collected supplies dropped from the air, and carried casualties back. When we can't get porters, a proportion of the fighting troops should be used as carriers. Porters must be trained to jungle conditions.

(g) Even good mule tracks can become impassable in the monsoon after heavy traffic due to deep mud. Nevertheless Jeep tracks can be kept going, given the labour, over most difficult routes.

(h) Men can move by night even on difficult tracks, but not off the tracks in the jungle, unless there is a good moon. Mules can negotiate difficult tracks by night, but cannot move through the jungle in the dark. A separate mule leader for each mule is necessary by night and over difficult tracks by day; infantry can be used temporarily as mule leaders over difficult stretches. Allow ample time for night moves.

(i) The value of Mae Wests for crossing streams.

(j) The value of a piece of phosphorescent wood on the back of the man in front of you.

(k) Air supply is possible even under the most difficult conditions of topography and weather. But time and labour are required to collect the supplies. Different coloured parachutes for ammunition and supplies are essential.

(l) Men, who have to remain continually in wet boots, get soft and sore feet very quickly. Anti-mosquito cream proved an excellent preventative and even a cure in mild cases. The question of providing a suitable vaseline is being examined.

(m) What to take and what to leave behind. See appendix A.

<u>Defence Against Air Attack</u>

Many of us have now experienced air attack. It is alarming but surprisingly ineffective, if precautions are taken. Inexperienced troops must be trained to stick it and must be taught how harmless it is by those who have experienced it. Most important of all, use every weapon to fire back at aircraft <u>in range</u>. The fact of hitting back is the best means of ensuring good morale. Explain to the troops that aircraft do not often actually crash when hit, because it is not easy to hit them in a vital spot. But Jap aircraft are not armoured, and no low flying aircraft should get away without several bullets through it; that will mean at the best a crash and at the worst several hours in workshops before it can be flown again.

In the jungle the best defence is concealment. If not spotted, <u>keep still</u>. Don't fire if you have not been located. Aircraft may fly over you in the hope that you will give away your position by firing. We have succeeded several times in locating Jap defences in this way because the Japs had not learnt to hold their fire. But if located shoot back for all you know.

Air sentries will always be posted – slit trenches always dug. On the alert sounding men will walk quietly to their trenches and be ready to fire at any place in range. Only if bombs are dropping may men double to their trenches.

On the move in M.T., keep moving and shoot back at the attacking plane. On the move on foot, keep motionless in the shadow of trees or buildings, but if you have been located, shoot back.

<u>Battle procedure and battle drills.</u>

The objects of both battle procedure and battle drill are:—

(a) to save time, and

(b) to ensure that, under the various sets of circumstances covered by these procedures and drills, each unit, sub-unit and individual knows exactly the action expected of him and it, and knows the action that will be taken by the co-operating units and individuals.

Battle procedure is the method by which commanders and their staffs co-ordinate and transmit in the shortest possible time orders for the executive action that is to be taken by units, sub-units and individuals.

Battle drill is the co-ordinated executive action taken by each unit, sub-unit and individual on receipt of certain words of command or signals.

A thorough knowledge of both battle procedure and battle drill is the basis of rapid manoeuvre and quick action in the field. Continual training in both is essential. A list of standard battle drills to be taught is given in appendix 'B'. The standard battle procedure now in use, involving the division of units into R, O, F and T groups, will be adopted for all the phases of battle including movement by M.T., movement by A.T. and harbouring.

We are training to fight in country similar to the Kabaw and Chindwin valleys. These areas include 'dense', 'thick' and 'thin' jungle, patches of open paddy fields, rivers varying in size from small chaungs to the Chindwin, and village areas often surrounded by paddy on all sizes.

Though we must be prepared for all types of country, training will be concentrate primarily on fighting in jungle, since jungle fighting is the most difficult to learn and since a high proportion of our fighting will take place in jungle. These Battle drills will be taught for 'thin' jungle (e.g. the teak forests of the Kabaw valley) with modifications for 'thick' jungle. These modifications will in general be a matter of distance only, since "visibility distance" is the ruling factor in jungle manoeuvre.

Health

Men cannot fight well unless they are fit and have confidence in their leaders. The welfare of his men must be uppermost in the mind of every leader from the section commander upwards. He must ensure that his men go into battle fresh and not hungry and that hot tea is available after the action or at the most convenient time. Special efforts must be made to provide rum after exposure to the wet or cold or severe strain. Leaders must take care of the health of their men including the care of their feet.

All leaders must study man management at all times. The pamphlet "The Handling of Men" will be read and re-read by all officers.

Men must be physically fit. But in training I do not want physical exertion to be carried to a state of exhaustion – no 40 or 50 mile marches on a few biscuits. If men are really physically fit, they will be able to endure hardships when the time comes.

Our sanitation has been good, but it can be better. Don't forget it on all occasions.

Transport
The transport reserves, both M.T. and A.T., in the division are being reduced in the new organization. Pooling of our resources will be even more necessary than before. Units must expect to be called upon to provide A.T. or M.T. or both at short notice.

Every unnecessary animal or vehicles that is kept forward merely adds to the difficulty of protection and supply. Send everything you don't want well to the rear. M.T. can be got forward again quickly when wanted. Every artillery mule must be got back on many occasions.

Animal Management
The need for, and the value of, good animal management was proved again and again. We have profited by experience and our animal management had been good, but there have been cases of neglect, in one case resulting in the loss of mules. Commanders are just as responsible for the welfare of their animals as they are for the welfare of their men.

Standing Instructions for Jungle Operations by a US Infantry Division on Guadalcanal
from *Notes from Theatres of War* 17: Far East, 1944

These instructions were issued by the commander of a US infantry division as a result of experience obtained in fighting the Japanese on GUADALCANAL. They present an admirable summary of the more important points of jungle fighting in the tropical conditions of the SW PACIFIC and are in agreement with British doctrine.

1. General.—The instructions contained herein, representing actual battle experience, will constitute a standing jungle operating procedure for units of this division. All members of the division will become thoroughly familiar with the instructions and comply therein.

2. Actions of individuals

(*a*) Weapons will be carried at all times when in forward areas and when away from immediate vicinity of bivouac, camps, or secured areas. Weapons will always be kept readily available.

(*b*) No lights of any kind will be used in forward positions during hours of darkness and no smoking unless specifically authorized by higher headquarters.

(*c*) Silence is essential at the front and on patrol. If the enemy can't locate you, every advantage is with you. He will try every means to get you to disclose your positions so that he can gain advantage over you.

(*d*) Don't shoot unless you have something worth while to shoot at. Blind shooting simply gives away your location and may kill your own comrades.

(*e*) Be on guard for all types of booby traps and other enemy ruses.

(*f*) Dig-in whenever halted and improve holes as time permits. An entrenching tool is next in value to a soldier's personal arms and must be carried at all times.

(*g*) Talk only in as low a tone as possible. Practise whispering especially in telephone conversations. Use signals, such as hand or arm signals, tapping on the rifle, bird calls, etc., as much as possible.

(*h*) Do not underestimate the enemy, but also do not overestimate him. The Japs are not supermen.

(*i*) Be on the lookout for false surrender; any offer of surrender must be suspected as an enemy ruse.

(*j*) Do not use field glasses openly; observe the same principles as in firing the rifle from concealment.

(*k*) Do not forget that many Japanese speak English. At night a favourite trick is for them to infiltrate and yell false orders; such as, "Withdraw," or "Serjeant, where are you?" Learn to know the voice of your leader. Japanese have difficulty in pronouncing the letter "l."

(*l*) Do not attempt to retrieve enemy wounded. It may be a trick.

(*m*) Do not forget to look up before you move. Get into the habit of watching tops of trees as well as their roots.

(*n*) Do not permit straggling, and do not straggle yourself.

(*o*) Rumours are a curse, don't start them or believe them and wait for verification.

(*p*) When fired on by snipers, move at top speed to nearest cover or concealment. As soon as possible quietly change your location, then locate and destroy the sniper. Do not, in any circumstances, stand still in the open.

3. Basic measures to counter Jap tactics

(*a*) The Japanese usually attack at night. Therefore our night positions must be organized for all-round defence by digging in, have a co-ordinated plan of automatic and mortar fire, and provide for strong security.

(*b*) In dense country the Japanese defend with limited fields of fire, with emplacements well dug in, using a high percentage of machine guns and snipers. Therefore, our best method of attack is to use flanking tactics with units working forward in small groups presenting small targets, using co-ordinated fire power or mortars, light machine guns, accurate rifle fire, hand grenades, demolitions, and the bayonet.

(*c*) The Japanese make extensive use of snipers, sometimes hidden in trees or tree roots, and invariably with limited fields of fire covering trails or open ground. Therefore, whenever possible, avoid trails and openings; study trees with field glasses, and when fired on by snipers, work around to get them from outside their line of fire.

In routing out snipers, especially in rear areas, the unit leader should assign a group of from three to six men to work on them, rather than have all the personnel engage in a fire-fight. In an advance, trees containing snipers should be flushed with machine-gun fire.

(*d*) All-round defence is imperative and must be habitual. Do not move without all-round security, and when you halt make that your first job.

(*e*) Always send at least two men on a mission, however simple the task may appear. Sentries must operate in pairs. There should be no relief or movements during the hours of darkness.

(*f*) Every effort will be made to capture prisoners. Send them at once under guard to the rear. They are the source of valuable information.

(*g*) It is imperative for morale that all officers maintain a cheerful and optimistic attitude, and that they do not show by word or action any discouragement or evidence of fatigue. Every officer must exhibit a desire for aggressive offensive combat, and instil the same desire in his men.

(*h*) Each platoon leader or other sub-unit leader will take every opportunity to instruct, talk over, discuss, and re-discuss with his men, Japanese tactics, our methods of operating against them, and will work out in detail the methods his unit will employ to get team work in their day and night operations against the enemy. It is essential that officers and men know and understand each other thoroughly.

4. Patrolling

(*a*) In both offensive and defensive operations in jungle country, extensive use will be made of patrolling. By maintaining constant pressure and contact with the enemy, he will be prevented from infiltrating forward and becoming organized and "set."

(*b*) Laying of ambushes on trails or near water holes has been an excellent method of harassing the Japanese and reducing their numbers.

(*c*) Each patrol will be carefully inspected and clear-cut instructions issued covering mission, objective, route or routes, adjoining patrols, formations, precautions, password, and signals. Helmets and web equipment will be camouflaged, shining equipment will be covered; all equipment must be adjusted so that it does not rattle or shine.

(*d*) Patrols will travel as lightly as possible, only the barest essentials being carried.

(*e*) Don't send a boy to do a man's job. Patrols will usually be assigned strengths as follows:—

    (i) Information only: a very small patrol, usually three to six men.

(ii) Combat, or reconnaissance in force, never less than a reinforced platoon, preferably larger.

(*f*) Formations will be adapted to the terrain, but must always provide all-round security by forward scouts, flank, and rear guards, with connecting groups. During a halt, whether for rest, observation, or bivouac, men will be kept dispersed and quiet, with alert sentinels and adequate security guards maintained. Remember you are always under observation and subject to machine gun or mortar fire if you present a suitable target.

(*g*) Do not attempt to move too rapidly. Make a thorough reconnaissance. Remember that false negative information is the most dangerous type. Commanders must estimate the time-factor and limit the extent of the patrol accordingly.

(*h*) Patrols will be provided with maps and sketches devoid of any military information. New trails and information of similar military value should be recorded on the spot and reports made immediately upon return to bivouac, and copies sent to division headquarters.

(*i*) Never halt in the open—select a concealed spot which affords cover and protection, except where such opening affords night security.

(*j*) Never permit a patrol to bunch up.

(*k*) Patrolling is easier and more successful when made during or immediately after rainfall.

5. Tactics

(*a*) Orders for an attack by a battalion or larger unit must be issued as early as possible. Reconnaissance in jungle operations requires much more time than in normal land operations.

(*b*) Whenever possible use flanking tactics. Most Japanese defensive positions are in the heavily wooded areas and ravines. Also, the Japanese prefer positions on the reverse slope of hills or ridges where they are defiladed from artillery fire. Enemy machine guns and sniper fire generally covers the crest of the ridge. They can usually be best attacked up, or down, the long axis of the ravine. An attack of this sort can make excellent use of mortar fire support.

(*c*) Experience indicates that about one-fifth of the fighting force of each battalion may have to be employed as carrying parties and to maintain the supply of ammunition, food, and water, and to handle the evacuation of casualties. This number should be kept at the minimum, and as soon as carrying parties are no longer needed they must be returned to the front.

(*d*) All surplus personnel and equipment not absolutely necessary for fighting must be left in the rear assembly area, to reduce fatigue of the fighting troops and to increase their mobility.

(*e*) Thorough consideration must be given to the possibilities of employing all supporting weapons and services available. Experience has shown that the Japanese machine gun and other weapons are so well emplaced that close heavy weapon support is necessary whenever the terrain permits.

(*f*) From the day before an attack each battalion taking part in it will have with it an artillery liaison officer and one or more artillery forward observers. They will be kept thoroughly informed of the plans for attack.

(*g*) Any reconnaissance that is detected will put the Jap on his guard. Either make reconnaissance undetected or reconnoitre in more than one locality to confuse the Jap as to your intentions.

(*h*) Do not permit supporting weapons, mortars and machine guns to clutter up and slow down advance elements in attack. Group them and move them up in rear by bounds.

(*i*) In attack through jungle advance slowly but surely. Do not rush in, then stop or fall back. Once forward movement has begun every effort must be made to continue that movement, however slow it may be.

6. Night operations

(*a*) When the attack on the Japanese extends into the afternoon, select the night position for your unit, dig in, and establish your co-ordinated defensive fire plan for all weapons before darkness.

(*b*) A covering force should be employed to prevent the enemy from having close-in observation of your main position.

(*c*) The Japanese attempt to locate our machine gun positions, so, if possible while your defensive position is being established, let the obvious locations be your dummy position and, just after darkness, move your machine guns to previously selected nearby primary positions. The Japanese plan their night attacks to take a limited objective (usually the position they see you occupy during daylight).

(*d*) The Japanese usually have their main attack directed at a flank. This is usually accompanied by a display of noise to our front. Under cover of this noise an advance echelon of men, carrying grenades, creep or crawl quietly up to our lines. Their mission is to throw grenades at our automatic weapons if we open fire prematurely at the noise created by the main body or demonstration forces. Therefore, never open fire at night at a noise.

(*e*) Limit movement at night to the absolute minimum.

(*f*) Cover luminous watches or other objects that will shine at night.

(*g*) For identification use the prescribed password. When challenging or replying to a challenge, speak quietly. Remember, the enemy has ears, too.

(*h*) Automatic weapons on fixed lines, grenades, and bayonets are the principal weapons for night use. Firing rifles at night usually causes casualties among friends as well as foes.

(*i*) Individual, or units, that are lost when night falls should select a covered position and remain for the night.

7. Equipment

(*a*) Individual equipment carried into combat in attack situations will include only absolutely essential items. Excess items hasten fatigue and lessen the mobility and fighting efficiency of attacking troops.

(*b*) Care of equipment will be strictly enforced. Do not let men get separated from their equipment. Unit leaders must ensure daily care of equipment.

(*c*) Darken any equipment to make it blend with tropical green, and dull items that might glisten or reflect light. Cover the canteen with a sack or cloth.

(*d*) Units must never leave equipment and supplies unguarded, even in rear areas.

8. Hygiene

(*a*) Since disease accounts for more casualties than bullets, it is imperative that every individual comply strictly with the following:—

    (i) Shallow trenches will be prepared whenever practicable. When not practicable, individuals will dig a small hole and cover excrement.

(ii) Slit trenches and other positions will be kept free of refuse.

(iii) All tins and surplus food must be buried.

(iv) Bedding will be sunned and aired whenever possible.

(*b*) Troops will be given every opportunity to bathe.

(*c*) Head nets will be worn at night unless the tactical situation prevents it. Clothing will be worn to cover body and limbs between dusk and dawn, the period when the malaria bearing mosquito is active. Gloves should be worn when appropriate.

(*d*) Special attention will be given to care of the feet to prevent blisters and "athlete's foot." Treat blisters and sores at first opportunity.

(*e*) Diarrhoea and dysentery are often caused by dirty mess tins. Mess tins will be thoroughly washed and cleansed in boiling water before each meal.

9. Signal communication

(*a*) Maximum use will be made of line communication, in preference to radio. Captured Jap wire can be used to supplement the supply of assault wire using ground return.

(*b*) Line will be repaired in daylight only, except in emergency. In laying line install one by fastest route, then a second on the return trip by a different route, raised high enough to be clear of traffic. Line parties in exposed forward areas will be protected by guards while at work.

Notes on Jungle Fighting
from *Current Reports from Overseas* 81

From a report from Burma

The following are, in my opinion, important points to watch in jungle fighting:—

(*a*) The need for strict discipline after striking camp.

(*b*) The need for good musketry training. A high standard of marksmanship and snap shooting up to 200 yards is required.

(*c*) The need for training in the use of No. 36 grenades with 4 second fuze, fired from the discharge cup to give air burst.

(*d*) The need for training in animal management. Mules are difficult to handle, and if they are to be kept going—as they must be—they have to be well cared for.

(*e*) The need for strict water discipline. Every man should be trained to do without water between sunrise and sunset; teach him to suck a pebble or chew gum instead.

(*f*) The need for every man to be A1 plus, and capable of marching 200 miles in 12 to 14 days.

(*g*) The need for the greatest care of feet. Australian socks do not shrink. South African made boots are the best.

(*h*) The need to prohibit smoking at night and to enforce absolute silence. Sound carried in the jungle, and speech should never rise above a whisper.

(*i*) The need for proficiency in the use of the compass, a high standard of map reading, and a knowledge of the stars for direction finding.

CHINDITS

Due to the disastrous retreat from Burma and First Arakan campaigns General Archibald Wavell, C-in-C India, brought over Brigadier Orde Wingate to India. Wavell wanted him to create a long range penetration group to operate behind the lines in in Japanese-occupied Burma relying on aerial supply and wireless contact. The first operation featured 77th Indian Infantry Brigade comprising battalions of the Burma Rifles, Gurkhas, the King's Liverpool Regt. and 142nd Commando Company. During Operation *Longcloth* the railway lines were cut a number of times between Mandalay and Myitkyina. More importantly, the troops involved emerged from the jungle as heroic figures lionised by the press as the first British and Commonwealth troops to get the better of the Japanese in the jungle, dispelling the myth of the Japanese 'Supermen'. The operation bolstered morale in both Britain and India. However only two thirds of the force made it back to India and of those only half were fit for duty again.

The second Chindit operation, Operation *Thursday,* began in March 1944. The formation had grown from a brigade in 1943 to almost the size of a small corps, comprising six brigades of 23,000 men to act as a long range penetration force. It was predominantly a British formation with Gurkhas, West Africans and Burma Rifles. Wingate disliked Indian Army officers and mistakenly thought Indian troops were not up to the same standards of the Chindits. For a short period of time he even commanded the 5307th Provisional Unit, an American infantry unit led by Brigadier General Frank Merrill and more commonly known as 'Merrill's Marauders'. The objective of the operation was threefold: to support Stilwell's advance into Myitkyina, encourage the Chinese forces from Yunnan to fight in northern Burma and as in the first operation attack the Japanese lines of communication. Five of the brigades were flown in and one went overland. Thence the brigades established strongholds from which columns would harass Japanese communications. On 24 March Wingate died in an air crash. He was replaced by Brigadier Lentaigne, an Indian Army officer, who was not a Wingate disciple and disagreed with many of his views on long range penetration tactics. The strongholds were attacked by the Japanese and these quickly became very attritional infantry battles that the Chindits were not trained or equipped for.

The Chindits displayed considerable powers of endurance during Operation *Thursday.* They had carried out the biggest behind-the-lines operation of the Second World War to date, involving some 20,000 men, and had lived and fought for five months under appalling conditions against the IJA, latterly carrying out operations increasingly of a conventional nature. The force was disbanded in February 1945. However, the lessons learnt by the Chindits were not forgotten and were passed on through a combination of cross-posting of officers and men as well as the transfer of the units. Indeed by 1945 the Fourteenth Army as a whole was employing air transportation, aerial re-supply and close air support on a hitherto unprecedented scale, in large part based on methods developed by Wingate and the Chindits.

The experience of the Chindits, the Fourteenth Army and General Stilwell's troops in Northern Burma showed that jungle training in India, based on the training pamphlets in this publication, was essential for success in the jungle. This was added to through battle experience in Burma. This recognition of the need for training in jungle fighting, a jungle warfare doctrine and extensive jungle experience in the Second World War aided the British Army in later campaigns in the Far East. For instance, during the Malayan Emergency, veterans of the Burma campaign formed Ferret Force, who were instrumental in tracking down Communist guerrilla camps in 1948 and served as instructors at the Jungle Warfare School in Johore.

Chindits in Action
from *Current Reports from Overseas* 85

(This selection contains a number of extracts from the written statements of officers who have at some time or another served with the Chindits.)

A night march in the jungle

"During the last Chindit operations in northern Burma the battalion in which I was serving was ordered to put down a road block on a certain road and to deny the use of the road to the enemy for forty-eight hours.

"Supplies had been dropped the day before, and we had collected a considerable quantity of ammunition and other stores. Owing to the fact that mules were our only form of transport and that they were already overloaded, it was necessary for every man to carry the stores required in the road block, as well as his normal load. Since each man's normal load after a supply drop was somewhere in the neighbourhood of eighty pounds, its carriage entailed a very considerable physical strain, especially as this load had to be humped about ten miles through the jungle by night. Personally, I was carrying, in addition to my normal load, one shovel, one cross-cut saw (shared with my batman), six grenades, fifty additional rounds of ammunition, and one chagul of water. My hands were full—in the strictest sense of the words.

"The battalion moved off at approximately 1500 hours. We were still some way from the objective when darkness fell and movement became more difficult.

"We had started out with the fighting group in front and the so-called 'soft' group, consisting of mules and administrative personnel, in rear. Since the route lay along jungle tracks it was necessary to move in single file and the battalion 'snake' must have been a mile or so long, consisting as it did of some 700 men and more than a hundred mules and ponies.

"At approximately 2230 hours the still of the night was shattered by confused shouts and considerable automatic fire from the rear of the column. The battalion was halted and the men, though handicapped by their heavy loads and considerably fatigued, took up positions of all-round defence.

"There were no further developments and the fighting group moved on for a quarter of a mile and waited for the tail of the column to catch up with it. After two hours had passed and there still was no sign of the administrative group, the commanding officer decided that it was impossible to put down the road block that night and sent back a strong fighting patrol to discover exactly what had happened. The patrol found the bodies of one officer and three other ranks and a number of dead Japanese. It was afterwards learnt that a gap had been allowed to develop between the fighting and administrative groups, and the latter, as it was passing through ha village, had been surprised and attacked by a patrol of some twenty Japanese armed with swords and automatic weapons. The situation had been saved by a serjeant-major who had swiftly organized a small party and driven off the enemy, inflicting considerable casualties upon them.

"The administrative group had proceeded to a pre-arranged rendezvous, where they met the rest of the battalion that night and the road block was duly put down next day. Nevertheless there was a lesson to be learnt from this operation, for it was realized that the men should not have been so overloaded as they were and, above all, that both hands should always be free to fight the enemy whenever and wherever he might appear.

"A word about morale. In penetration warfare, the incidence of physical fatigue is probably higher than in most other forms of warfare. There is also the considerable mental fatigue caused by the strain of operating behind the enemy's lines. I do not think that many of us were ever completely at our ease. For my part I found that having to keep one's voice to a whisper most of the time had a most adverse effect on morale—possibly out of all proportion to the usefulness of such an imposition."

The Last Encounter
from *Current Reports from Overseas* 86

(The following is a description by the column intelligence officer of an operation carried out by a long range penetration group in Burma.)

"In our very last encounter with the Japanese in September, 1944, we were once again reminded—if any reminder were necessary—that continual aggressiveness, which gives the enemy no chance to rest, will defeat him in the end, even though he is very strongly entrenched and determined to hold out at all costs.

"The scene was a dense stretch of jungle, through which ran a single track. Our objective was a village about a mile away. The intervening distance was studded with an intricate system of trench defences which the Japanese had dug some time before. Our men were very tired and the respective strengths of the two fighting companies were approximately 80 and 90 men, supported by four 3 inch mortars. We were attacking unknown defences, for satisfactory reconnaissance had been impossible owing to the thickness of the jungle, but the strength of the enemy was estimated at 60 or 70 men with a high proportion of automatic weapons.

"One company was first committed and the normal encircling tactics, preceded by a heavy mortar barrage, were employed. The mortar observation post, using both line and 'walkie-talkie', advanced with the company, and in all nearly 100 bombs were fired. The Japanese, as usual, refused to budge; every hole had to be cleared with bayonet or grenade. The enemy positions had been very well sited and it soon became obvious that the only way of pushing farther along the track was by wearing down the enemy by means of continuous infantry attack, supported by mortar concentrations. The assault took the form of one company leapfrogging through another, each company with all the mortars in support.

"It took us three days to clear the track, and even then success was achieved only by the dash and dogged persistence of our continuous attack that gave the enemy no rest; no sooner had he relinquished one position than he was again attacked before he could properly take up another. The mortars were invaluable and there is no doubt but that they had a devastating effect upon the enemy's morale, besides inflicting numerous casualties. The infantry fighting was carried out at very close quarters (10 to 15 yards), and towards the end of the operation we put in two bayonet charges, neither of which the enemy would face. Indeed, the second bayonet assault completely broke their spirit; they packed up and ran and, in running, conceded the last two hundred yards of their defences.

"Our losses were four men killed and four wounded. Had we sat down and decided to take our time over each of the enemy defence systems, casualties would probably have amounted to twelve times that number, and we should have been hard at it to this day. 'Keep at 'em' was our motto. It was the right one."

SOURCES

CHAPTER 1: DOCTRINE

Military Training Pamphlet No. 9 (India): The Jungle Book (India Army General Staff, 4th Edition, September 1943), Chapters I–XII

Field Manual 72-20: Jungle Warfare (War Department, 27 October 1944), Chapter 3: I, II

CHAPTER 2: LIVING IN THE JUNGLE

'The Jungle Lane to teach jungle lore', *Army in India Training Memorandum No. 25* (India Army General Staff, July 1944) and *Jungle Jottings 1945* (The War Office, July 1945)

'Uses of bamboo', *Military Training Pamphlet 52: Warfare in the Far East* (The War Office, 1944) (also in *The Jungle Book*)

MTP No. 9 (India): The Jungle Book (1943), Chapter XIII

'Food available in the Jungle', *Tactical and Technical Trends* 21 (Military Intelligence Service, War Department, 25 March 1943)

'Drinking Water from the Rattan Vine', *Tactical and Technical Trends* 34 (Military Intelligence Service, War Department, 23 September 1943)

FM 72-20: Jungle Warfare (1944), Appendix I: Native Plants

Malaria, 1943, A Pamphlet for Officers (The War Office, January 1943)

Medical Problems in Jungle Warfare and the Pacific Warfare (US Command and General Staff School, 10 May 1945)

MTP No. 9 (India): The Jungle Book (1943), Chapter XIII

FM 72-20: Jungle Warfare (1944), Chapter 3: III, IV

'Camouflage in Jungle Warfare', *Notes from Theatres of War* 17: Far East, 1944 (The War Office, May 1944), accessed National Archives, WO 208/3108

Soldier's Guide to the Japanese Army (Military Intelligence Service, War Department Washington, 15 November 1944), Chapter VI, Jungle Warfare

'Appendix B: Japanese Ruses', *Notes from Theatres of War* 19: Burma 1943/1944 (The War Office, May 1945), accessed National Archives, WO 208/5637

CHAPTER 3: LEARNING THE LESSONS

Battle Instructions for Jungle Fighting (23 Indian Division, September 1944), accessed National Archives, WO 203/2475

'Standing Instructions for Jungle Operations by a US Infantry Division on Guadalcanal', *Notes from Theatres of War* 17: Far East, 1944 (The War Office, 21 March 1945), accessed National Archives, WO 208/3108

'Notes on Jungle Fighting', *Current Reports from Overseas* 81 (The War Office, 21 March 1945), accessed National Archives, WO 208/3111

'Chindits in action', *Current Reports from Overseas* 85 (The War Office, 25 April 1945), accessed National Archives, WO 208/3111

'The Last Encounter', *Current Reports from Overseas* 86 (The War Office, 9th May 1945), accessed National Archives, WO 208/3111 .